Toth Alexis

Where to Seek the Truth?

Toth Alexis

Where to Seek the Truth?

ISBN/EAN: 9783744763059

Printed in Europe, USA, Canada, Australia, Japan

Cover: Foto ©Lupo / pixelio.de

More available books at **www.hansebooks.com**

ARCHIVES OF AMERICANS OF RUSSIAN DESCENT IN MINNESOTA

3217 - 32ND AVE. N.E. MINNEAPOLIS, MN. 55418 USA

The Writings of St. Alexis Toth,
Confessor and Defender of Orthodoxy
in America

TRANSLATED AND EDITED BY

GEORGE SOLDATOW

AARDM PRESS MINNEAPOLIS, MINNESOTA
1994

HOLY FATHER ALEXIS, CONFESSOR AND DEFENDER OF ORTHODOXY
IN AMERICA

3

LIST OF ABBREVIATIONS

APV - Amerikanskii Pravoslavnyi Viestnik

AARDM - Archives of Americans of Russian Descent in Minnesota.
Established in 1975. Included some unique documents and
manuscripts and also secondary source materials by and
about Russian immigrants to the state. Also included some
materials by and about Ukrainians and the largest collection
of materials in Minnesota about the Carpathians (Rusins).

ARV - Amerikanskii Russkii Viestnik

NOTES

* - Indicates a footnote by the editor.

First Workers in Newly Constructed Church
1900

Prof. Michael Perhach, Choirmaster,   Very Rev. Archpriest Alexis G. Toth, Pastor,   John Repa — President of Church Committee

INTRODUCTION

St. Alexis was born in Carpathia (Hungarian Empire) in 1854. He came from a poor gentry family distinguished for its piety. His father and his brother were priests and his uncle was a bishop in the Uniate Church.

St. Alexis was ordained in 1878 after he married Rosalie Michalich, a priest's daughter, and was appointed as a second priest to a Uniate parish. St. Alexis was highly educated and knew several languages, serving before his priestly appointment as secretary in the Ecclesiastical Administration of the Presov diocese.

However it seems that the Lord planned a different future for St. Alexis than to be a bureaucrat or a professor. Soon after his ordination his wife and thereafter their only child died leaving him alone in grief with his parents.

In 1879, he was appointed as secretary to the Bishop of Presov and as manager of the Diocesan Administration. He did not serve long in this capacity; after only two years he was appointed a Professor of the Theological Academy in Presov to teach Church Law and Church History. At the same time he had to fulfill the duties of Director of an orphanage. Then in 1883 the Diocesan Administration assigned him to fulfill the priestly obligations in an Art school in addition to his other responsibilities.

In October of 1889 St. Alexis was appointed as a missionary to North America to be the pastor of a Uniate parish in Minneapolis, Minnesota. Upon his arrival in Minneapolis in December, he went to introduce himself to the local Roman Catholic Archbishop, John Ireland, since the Uniates were part of the Roman Catholic Church. The Archbishop did not want to have any parishes of non-Roman rite in the United States and was outraged by the arrival of St. Alexis, a widowed Uniate priest, for that parish. Bishop Ireland disregarded all agreements which had been made by Rome with the Uniates and refused to acknowledge or allow any ifferences from the Roman Rite. As a result there was a heated discussion between Ireland and St. Alexis and he was denied jurisdiction in his parish.

The views of Archbishop Ireland were shared by other Catholic bishops in America. This meeting between Ireland and St. Alexis was typical of the reception given to other Uniate priests by Roman Catholic Bishops throughout America. The Catholic hierarchy also had problems in North America with Roman Catholics who were Poles, Czechs, etc. and not Irish or Anglo-Saxon. It was not a misunderstanding but systematic resistance by the Irish Bishops to petitions from these people for parish clergy of their own nationality, to keep their national identity within the Church. Some of these groups formed their own Catholic Dioceses, independent from the American Catholic Church, which were and are directly administered from Rome or built their independent Unions such as the Old-Catholic Churches in America.

Until the time of the arrival of St. Alexis in America, the Catholic Church in the United States had been the beneficiary of European assistance. The church in the United States was not in a strong financial position and depended on donations. In 1908 Pope Pius X removed the United States from the missionary jurisdiction of the Congregation of Propaganda and incorporated the American Church into the ordinary administration of the universal Roman Catholic Church.

The Roman Pontiffs and the Curia had the idea of uniting all Christians around the Roman Pope and as a result made various agreements with the Greeks, Eastern European and Middle Eastern Orthodox, and other Christians. The Catholic Bishops in America did not have the same plans and therefore a long process of disagreements began between them and the Roman Curia.

St. Alexis was not an ordinary priest. He knew his rights as a Uniate. He was a natural leader who was more educated than other priests who came from Carpathia, and he had a knowledge of Church history and law.

Before St. Alexis' arrival in Minneapolis, his parishioners had already built and blessed their church (without permission from Bishop Ireland). After his meeting with the Bishop, St. Alexis tried to work within the terms of the agreement between the Uniates and the Roman Catholics and the rules established by Rome concerning his ministry in America. In 1890 he called a meeting of Uniate priests in America in Wilkes-Barre, Pennsylvania. There were al that time 10 Uniate priests in the United States and 8 of them came to the meeting. St. Alexis was elected as their chairman. The meeting dealt mainly with answering the challenges faced by the Uniate Church in America. St. Alexis was instrumental in bringing together the Uniate priests in America but neither the Uniate Bishops in Carpathia nor Rome came to their assistance, heard their suffering or sent a Uniate Bishop to administer the parishes in North America. St. Alexis had great plans for his people in America and in 1890 alone he traveled from Minneapolis to visit Uniate immigrants in distant places including Chicago and Streator, Illinois; Cleveland, Los Angeles, Galveston, the state of Alabama, St. Louis, the state of Dakota, Ashland (Wisconsin), and several places in Canada. He called upon the people to form fraternities, to build churches. He wished to unite all fraternities into one Mutual Aid Society.

At the same time Archbishop Ireland continued his attacks against St. Alexis and his parishioners. In Catholic churches condemnations were read; parishioners were told not to listen to or even contact St. Alexis. St. Alexis and his people did not know what they should do in these circumstances; they had a meeting and came to what St. Alexis called " something that was long in my heart". St. Alexis and his parishioners decided to seek a way to return to the jurisdiction of an Orthodox Bishop rather than a Roman Catholic or Uniate Bishop. It is important to emphasize, that this first return to Orthodoxy by an entire parish and its pastor occurred without any influence from the Orthodox Church Administration, which was unaware of these people in America. It was in accordance with the decision of the parishioners themselves. They came from a territory that was part of Kievan Rus'; they had never been part of the Muscovite Rus' and they had been Uniates. This petition was completely unexpected by the Russian Orthodox Church and it took a long time before the Russian Synod accepted this parish into the diocese. But after the first Uniate parish was reunited, it became a mission to attract other parishes and that was where St. Alexis was instrumental.

It is obvious that St. Alexis was not a "revolutionary" or a priest who disobeyed his Church authorities. He was appointed by his Bishop to go to America and to give spiritual guidance to people from his homeland; but his right to do that was disregarded and denigrated by a local Bishop not even of his jurisdiction. A Union meant that Roman Catholics and Uniates were able to keep their differences as they were before the Union and the only condition was that both groups would be under the spiritual guidance of the Pope in Rome. Therefore Bishop Ireland and other American Bishops were in disagreement with the Papal Church and Administration and not St. Alexis who in spite of all his difficulties, would not return to Carpathia abandoning his own people, violating his (and other clergy's) belief in the right of Unia and of the equality of Eastern and Western Rites in the Church. Saint Alexis followed his own conscience as to the best way to preserve the faith; the only way he found was to reunite, with his parish, to Orthodoxy rather than to continue to be misinformed, dominated and fooled by his supposed equality with Roman Catholic priests.

After the Hungarian Revolution of 1848, the life of the Carpathian people, including those in Galicia which had been added to the Empire after the Polish partition, was barely tolerable. The Austrian Emperor was crowned King of Hungary and the Hungarian government treated all of those in their territory as Hungarians and Roman Catholics. Previously, there had been difficulties with Roman Catholic clergy, who sought to force the Uniates to accept Western traditions and newly introduced Roman Catholic doctrines. After the establishment of an independent Hungarian government with authority over the Carpathian regions, the civil authorities attempted to enforce these changes. Many other problems within the Hungarian Kingdom encouraged people to emigrate. Czechs, Slovaks and Carpathians all wished to have autonomy in their political and cultural lives and there were also economic difficulties.

It has to be noted, that a large percentage of people from Carpathia came to the United States. Many villages lost half of their population or most of the young people due to emigration to North America. Only about one third of the people over 14 years of age who emigrated to the United States were literate. Many of these literate people were not well educated, and therefore needed not only spiritual but cultural guidance that they could receive only from their own priests. Uniate bishops sent priests to North America for their people for these needs.

Many of these people had the opinion that they were Orthodox, as was the case with Mr. Mlinar, who was delegated by the parish in Minneapolis to go to the Russian Orthodox Bishop Vladimir in San Francisco. Bishop Vladimir sent him to the Roman Catholic Bishop who sent Mr. Mlinar back to the Orthodox Bishop. As a result poor Mr. Mlinar wrote to St. Alexis asking him "What kind of a faith do we have? I have never heard of Uniates. All priests told us that we were Orthodox Christians!!!"

After Mr. Mlinar returned to Minneapolis, St. Alexis went to meet Bishop Vladimir and there in the Cathedral in San Francisco was reunited with the Orthodox Church. In March of 1891, the Bishop came to Minneapolis and reunited the parishioners with the Orthodox Church. It was not until July 14, 1892 that the Russian Synod decided to accept St. Alexis and his parish into the Aleutian Diocese and to give St. Alexis a salary like that of other Orthodox priests in North America. Before that St. Alexis worked in a bakery, at the same time fulfilling his priestly obligations. The acceptance into the Orthodox Diocese was a great relief for St. Alexis and his people, who had suffered all kinds of vicious accusations and threats. After this event t here were, however, other accusations of St. Alexis for "selling his people and religion to the 'Moscovites". Rumors were spread of astronomical sums that he had received from Moscow. In reality St. Alexis was living without financial support from anyone including his parish in Minneapolis which was at that time very poor.

After being accepted into the Orthodox Diocese, St. Alexis called upon all Uniates and their clergy, that he had visited before in North America to join him and to reunite with the Holy Orthodox Church. He became instrumental in the return and formation of 17 Orthodox parishes in North America. He helped not only Carpathians, but also Russians, Galicians and other Orthodox people to establish parishes. As a result of his call to the Carpathian people, during the next several decades many more thousands of Carpathian Uniates returned to Holy Orthodoxy, the Faith of their fathers, forming more than 300 parishes across North America. St. Alexis became their first and most effective missionary and they called him "Bat'ko" - Father. There were after him many other Orthodox missionaries in North America but only one was called "Bat'ko" by the Carpathians.

St. Alexis was a highly educated priest, but in his teaching, he used language and subjects that his people could understand. He simplified his theological teaching for these people since they were not prepared to go into dogmatic details. He received from the Orthodox Diocesan Administration the assignment to go to different places and to teach Orthodoxy and form people into parishes. In one of his letters to another Orthodox priest who was in the Administration, St. Alexis wrote that there is so much that he himself has to learn and he tries, but he has to spend all of his time for missionary work.

It is possible that St. Alexis made some errors in his sermons and his teaching, but it seems that they were neither many nor great. As Fr. Hopko wrote in his book "The Orthodoxy": A heretic brings disagreement and damage into the Church, he acts intentionally. Fr. Hopko wrote: even in the teachings of the Holy Fathers there are things that were later accepted as inexact or false, but these Holy people are not counted as heretics. As the Holy Orthodox Church teaches, only God does not make errors and is infallible. St. Alexis, even if he did make mistakes in his teachings, made them unintentionally.

Rev. Bishops Vladimir and Nicholas were Christ's Bishops, representing Him in America, and therefore Fr. Alexis, receiving a direct order to go and teach in all places where there were Carpathian people, had to obey their orders. St. Alexis did not respond, that he is not ready to do this work or that he wishes to do something else. It often happened that receiving a mission, people found, like Moses did, all kinds of excuses, but that was not the case with St. Alexis. For all the results of his missionary activity he has to be accepted as the greatest Orthodox missionary in North America among the East European immigrants. Mostly St. Alexis was the only one defending the Orthodox Church from the Uniate attacks, since other clergy were busy building churches in their parishes, collecting funds, teaching in the Missionary School and in the Seminary, editing the newspaper, the magazine, the calendar etc, and St. Alexis was left alone to answer the accusations that appeared in the press. For that reason the Orthodox Church in America considers St. Alexis as Defender of Orthodoxy in America.

St. Alexis had a vision of all Orthodox people of all nationalities in North America united around one Orthodox Bishop, with equality among these national groups who would "in this free country be able to glorify the Lord in their own language". When asked by Bishop Tikhon to express his opinion about how the Orthodox Church should be registered in its charter, St. Alexis wrote a long report examining all possibilities. He proposed a "Greek-Catholic Church of America standing under the Spiritual Jurisdiction of the Holy Governing Synod of Russia", but as he pointed out, according to the American judicial view the members should be then only Greeks and Russians. As the only good solution he suggested "Orthodox Church of (changed by St. Tikhon to "in") America, since its members were not only Greeks and Russians but Arabs, Syrians, Serbians, Slovaks, Hungarians, Americans, and Indians".

From the beginning of his mission St. Alexis wrote articles in local immigrant publications. He defended Orthodoxy. He pointed out the misguided position of the Roman Catholics who followed the new dogmatic teaching of Papal Infallibility; he accused them of not fulfilling their obligations to all Uniates and especially those in America. He called upon Orthodox people to use Orthodox terminology such as Pascha, not Easter and Nativity of Christ instead of Christmas. Christmas, he pointed out, is a Roman Catholic name, coming from a Mass to Christ. Orthodox people do not have a Mass but a Liturgy. Besides that Christmas is only the word in the English language; in other countries this holy day is called differently.

His publications appeared in different languages. For example in a Slovak newspaper he published an article in Slovak "How we should live in America". In this article he tells that this is a land of freedom, but people should live here according to local laws and standards. He suggests that people should change the behavior and habits that they used in the old country. He says that people should keep their houses clean, wash their children and clean the windows; even in poverty people can live in cleanliness. He compares the Slavs with English people and suggests to parents that they send their children to school instead of sending them to work in mines or other places. St. Alexis especially warns people of the danger of alcoholism, especially when young people start to drink alcohol. He instructs that people should not sing, shout or holler in the streets.. He teaches them "to hold on to your faith teaching and do not attack the faith of others". Respect other people... read good religious and national books, especially on Sunday, instead of drinking. "Read a good newspaper, those will teach you how to be a good Christian and a good nationalist, read "The Life of Jesus Christ", "The Virgin Mary", and other books..." "Apply for and take citizenship papers if you wish to live here". He teaches how women should be treated in America, that they should dress decently, and not go barefoot in the street, dressed in peasant costumes, etc.

Right after he became pastor first in Minneapolis and later in Wilkes-Barre, St. Alexis started local church schools where he and his assistants taught religion, language and other subjects. He was instrumental in the opening of schools in other Orthodox parishes. He also taught adults, not just children.

It was his idea that it was important for the Orthodox Church in America to have a publication. As a result of his correspondence with Bishop Nikolas, "Svet" (Light) began publication and Fr. Hrushka, a former Uniate priest and friend of St. Alexis became its editor.

St. Alexis' most famous and influential book "Where to Seek the Truth" was written by the end of 1893. It was directed to Slavic people from the Austro-Hungarian Empire and was written in a simple question and answer format. It gave the readers basic information about the origin and place of Christianity, how it spread, the Ecumenical Councils, heresies and schism and the reasons for them. St. Alexis indicates that the mission of the Church is the guidance of people to salvation. In his book the saint answered such questions as "Can we call the Pope Christ's successor? Did Christ, the Apostles, the Holy Fathers, or the Ecumenical Councils teach or write any-thing about infallibility?" The book explained the basic differences and origins of Orthodoxy, Roman Catholicism, Protestantism and Unia, but indicates that the only true way of salvation is through Orthodoxy.

This book of St. Alexis was written in simple and understandable language for people who came from villages in Carpathia, Galicia and Bukovina. It was accepted by these people with joy and influenced many at a time when there was no other available and easily understandable religious literature. Therefore St. Alexis' work was unique and has great merit to the Church as labor of Enlightenment and preaching of the Gospel.

It can be observed that in his writings and sermons St. Alexis expressed his devotion to the Russian Church, Russia and its Czar. He defended all of them because he believed that they were the only protectors and supporters of other Orthodox people around the world. His love for Russia was not in conflict with his loyalty to his new country, the United States. He said many times, that it was only because of the freedom in the United States that he and his followers enjoyed and were able to fulfill their wish to become Orthodox.

St. Alexis had his unique methods of preaching. For example after receiving an order from the Most Holy Synod in Russia concerning acceptance to the Aleutian Diocese, he tells the parishioners in his sermon: "Orthodox Christians! ... we were detached for 244 years from our Mother Church... the Church of Christ, the only Holy Ecumenical and Apostolic Church... We suffered much here being Uniates from those who told us that we were one of a whole with them... I have informed you about the Church's teach- teaching... and now you have to live with goodness, peaceful Christian lives, in love to the Lord and His Church proving that not only in words but in your hearts and deeds we are true children of the Orthodox Church,- God and the Orthodox Church will not leave us, and the Lord's love will be among us forever! Amen..."

In another sermon he tells people that the Holy Virgin was always the Protector of Orthodox Christians. She protected cities from attacks by infidels, for example the city of Azov. Almost every city glorifying the Theotokos had its own icon; many of them were known as miraculous. He spoke about the special bond between the Orthodox people and the Theotokos, of many holy days and many churches that are dedicated to Her glorification.

In another sermon to the people of Old Forge, Pennsylvania, on the occasion of their return to the Orthodox Church, St. Alexis spoke about people suffering for the Orthodox Faith in Austrian and Hungarian Kingdoms and about the faults of Unia. He told people to hear what the Orthodox Church preaches and not what others tell about Orthodoxy; for example, that the Orthodox people do not believe in the Holy Trinity or the Theotokos.

In his sermons St. Alexis told the Uniates, that the Uniate Church is not Roman Catholic nor Orthodox, but that it became a mixture of both, that the people are now ashamed of. Hear the Orthodox teaching, said he, "this is the teaching of the Christian Orthodox Church, this is the teaching of your forefathers, your fathers, this is your faith, through which all of us will come to salvation. Hold to it! Amen."

It seems that St. Alexis was guided by the Lord; he came at the right time and right place to the defense and mission of Orthodoxy in America, becoming its champion. For his achievements St. Alexis became not only Defender but also Confessor of Orthodoxy in America. His teaching has influenced not only people here in America but also in the Carpathian homeland. The return to Orthodoxy spread there also. For this reason it can be said that St. Alexis had the virtue of service to the Fatherland.

St. Alexis had many other virtues, such as those of self sacrifice and unselfishness. As an example, for years he asked the Bishop's permission to go for a visit to his mother in Hungary, but he stayed each time when the Bishop indicated how much there was to be done for the Church and its people. When he was offered the leadership of his people in America as a Bishop, with humility he pointed out that this responsibility should be given to a younger and healthier man than he, who would be more effective to the Glory of God.

The doors to St. Alexis' house were always open to anyone who was looking for assistance and advice. His limited funds were shared with other clergy and given to needy people. In his "Last Will", he wrote: "Let my funeral be simple, without pomp and wreaths, and the casket as cheap as possible. Eulogies need not be said; otherwise, let every one pray for my soul which stands in fear before God's Judgment Throne. Wealth I have none..." Saint Alexis' life insurance and savings covered only part of his debts. To his relatives and friends he left very little, only small things as mementos. He left a little fund for prayers for his parents. His entire estate was determined at $5498.45 against $6529.84 of claims against his estate.

He spent much of his income for the defense of the church in Wilkes-Barre from the Uniates and Roman Catholics, and then, after the church burned down, for building a new one on the same place. He donated for the education of seminarians in Minneapolis and to schools. He helped many people in every way that he could.

When St. Alexis was offended or fooled by other people, in his love he forgave them and always asked his Bishop to forgive him his omissions and mistakes.

He helped much in building Orthodox churches in America, giving his advice in different parishes, and helping to collect funds for the church buildings.

St. Alexis' teaching was in accordance with the Orthodox Ecumenical Councils and Church canons. In some instances there are signs of his national pride but that is excusable since it was in conjunction with his defense of the Church. In some cases his comments might seem harsh or inappropriate. It has to be remembered that he taught in language common to the time and the meaning of some words have changed since then. Also, of course, was the fact, that many of his comments were responses to unfounded accusations of Orthodoxy and the Mission in North America by people who used much stronger language than St. Alexis and unethical methods of discrediting them; a lack of tolerance, rude behavior and threats against his people. St. Alexis may in fact only be commended, for his restraint. It also should not be forgotten that many of St. Alexis' strong comments appeared only in private correspondence with the church administration. Some people that he wrote about were indeed, as the future showed, revolutionaries. St. Alexis was not wrong in his evalua- tions about their plans against the Church.

As described above, St. Alexis had merits to the Orthodox Church in America, he was a defender of the Orthodox Faith, his mission was not only in North America but was spread even to his own Homeland by people returning there; he helped to build churches, he had a lot of patience, and sacrificed much for the Church, he was unselfish, humble and loved other people, he was a laborer of Enlightenment to his people, a theologian, a teacher and preacher. St. Alexis endured such suffering and persecution from Uniates, a hostile press, enemies of the Church and representatives of the Hungarian Empire, that he might even be considered a martyr for the Faith. St. Alexis for his exceptional merits of service to the Church was awarded by the Most Holy Synod with an epigonation, a Miter and the title of Archpriest. At that time these were quite rare awards given by the Church only to exceptionally distinguished priests. From civil authorities in Russia he received also 2 orders of each St. Ann and St. Vladimir 4 th and 3 rd class for his services for the Red Cross in Japan, for Fraternities, in the Mutual Aid Society, in orphanages, for the newspaper, parish libraries and education in America. In his memory and in veneration, right after his death an orphanage in Vermont was dedicated in his name and members of the Orthodox Church of America ordered a splendid mausoleum built in his memory in the Saint Tikhon monastery. His death did not stop the spreading of his achievements and his work was continued by such dedicated workers as Rev. Fr. Peter Kohanik and others, who said that they were continuing what St. Alexis began.

The grounds for canonization of saints has varied during the history of the Holy Orthodox Church, since in each particular case of glorification specific reasons might be found which depended both on the feat performed by the zealot for salvation and on those spiritual requirements which the Orthodox Church deemed necessary to make for the sake of the goodness and salvation of her believers in different periods of history. Glorification varied in different Orthodox national churches also. The Church in any case has considered the feat performed and then pronounced its decision. They study the life, miracles and labors performed by the zealots proposed for canonization. Their various deeds of spiritual perfection illuminate a path for salvation for the present day Orthodox people.

The Ecumenical Patriarch Dimitrios and the Greek Archdiocese praised St. Alexis' achievements and the Carpatho-Russian Diocese holds him in great veneration. St. Alexis was a member of the Church that has become the Orthodox Church in America; he worked to build this Church and he shared the vision of "One Holy Orthodox Church", guided in this country by one Pastor, for all ethnic groups. St. Alexis' is with this Church today; his life and achievements are clearly visible. The story of St. Alexis' life reads like a story of a true Apostle, endless traveling, labors, great sacrifices and constant persecution from the enemies of Orthodoxy. Therefore the honor of his glorification as a Saint was expected to be made by the Orthodox Church in America.

Why is there such a great interest in St. Alexis? The reason is that today, as before faith is being tested in the crisis of religious tensions and in contemporary society. The Orthodox Church needs help from above and from leadership such as that of St. Alexis, to face the challenges of secular values. Saint Alexis shows how it was possible to reflect our precious Orthodox Faith and share it with others.

This volumes includes translations from Russian to English of selected articles, his work "Where to seek the truth" and selected sermons in the belief that, although published a long time ago, the problems that they deal with are still in existence today. The text was followed as closely as possible, retaining the long sentences and somewhat confused phraseology often characteristic of St. Alexis' writings. To have eliminated these, and to have translated the whole freely in a different style would have destroyed the character of his writing. In some places the incorrect phraseology, as well as the grammatical mistakes, could not be preserved in translation without losing St. Alexis' meaning. Where possible, the original punctuation marks and paragraph structure have been preserved. The spelling of personal names sometimes varied; where variances occurred, the name has been standardized by the way it appeared in print in the court record, a newspaper or other printed material. Complete personal names are retained as much as posible. It was often necessary to add some additional material in the form of footnotes to further illuminate St. Alexis' activities or explain Orthodox teaching. At the end of the volume there is the Proclamation of the Holy Synod of the Orthodox Church in America on the Glorification of the Holy and Righteous Archpriest Alexis Toth and the Service to St. Alexis, Confessor and Defender of Orthodoxy in America.

George Soldatow

10

WHERE TO SEEK THE TRUTH ?

1. Who established the Christian Faith?
   Jesus Christ, the Son of God, the Savior of the world, God, and Man.
2. Where was Jesus Christ born?
   In the East, in the Judean city of Czar David - Bethlehem, of the Most Holy
   Virgin Mary (Micheas 5:2, Matt. 2:6).
3. Where did Christ live, teach, suffer, die, rise from the dead, ascend to Heaven,
   and to where did He send the Holy Spirit?
   In the East - in Jerusalem.
4. Where was the term Christian first used?
   In the East - in Antioch.
5. From what place did the Christian Faith spread to the entire world?
   From the East - from Jerusalem.
6. Where was the first Christian Church?
   In the East - in Jerusalem.
7. Where did the Ecumenical Councils meet?
   In the East in the cities of Nicaea, Constantinople, Chalcedon, and Ephesus.[1]
8. Where did the greatest Holy Fathers of Christ's Church live?
   In the East - such Fathers as St. Basil the Great, St. John Chrysostom, St.
   Athenasius, St. Gregory, St Nicholas the Miraclemaker, and others.
9. From where did our ancestors the Russians accept Christianity?
   From the East - Czargrad (Constantinople).[2]
10. From where did the Apostles of the Slavs, Sts. Methdius and Cyril, come?
    From the East - from Czargrad.
11. Where is the Christian Faith preserved in its purity, unchanged even in our time?
    In the East and also in those countries which have accepted Christian teaching
    from the East - such as Russia, Greece, Rumania, and Serbia; in Hungary among
    the Serbians and Romanians, and in Bukovina among the Russians (Rusins).
12. What is that Faith called?
    Orthodox-Catholic, or Greek-Russian.
13. What does the word Orthodox mean?
    It means a person, or a church, or a nation, with right-correct beliefs according to the
    true Faith in God, and the keeping of the Lord's laws and orders in the way that Christ
    Himself, His Apostles, the Holy Fathers, and the Seven Holy Ecumenical Councils taught
    and commanded.

---

[1]* The Seven Ecumenical Councils:

Nicaea	- 325
Constantinople	- 381
Ephesus	- 431
Chalcedon	- 451
Constantinople II	- 553
Constantinople III	- 680
Constantinople IV	- 754
Nicaea II	- 787

These Councils formulated the basic Christian doctrine, by witnessing to and defining truths of
revelation, and by shaping forms of worship and discipline. In general, they represented attempts
by the Church to mobilize itself in times of crisis for self-defence, self-purification and growth.
They condemned heresies, formulated the Creed, and condemned Iconoclasm.

[2] *The Russians also call Constantinople "Czargrad" - the city of the Czar, the supreme autocrat of
all Christians. After the fall of that city to the Moslems, Constantinople's authority and responsibilities were transferred to Moscow which became known as the "Third Rome".

14. What does the word "catholic" mean?

This word is Greek and it means "sobornyi"[3]

15. Why is the Orthodox Faith also called "Greek'?

Because the first rituals of the Faith were established in the Greek language, then three of the first Evangelists, St. John, St. Luke and St. Mark wrote the Holy Gospel, only St. Matthew wrote it in Hebrew.[4] St. Apostle Paul, St. Peter, St. Jacob, the Holy Fa thers and the Holy Ecumenical Councils were written and conducted only in Greek. In this language they taught the Faith; and the reason is that the Greek language is very enlightened and very beautiful. The Holy Scripture in Latin appeared in the third century, that is 300 years after Christ's birth. Our Savior in His earthly life did not speak or teach in Latin.[5]

16. And why is the Orthodox Faith also called "Russian"?

Because this Faith is confessed by the most glorious, greatest and most religious people, the Russians; it is missionized by the great, glorious, mighty Russia where more than 80 million people are Orthodox.

1. **Remark**: From all of the above it is obvious that the salvation of humankind, and the preservation of everything that is good and beneficial for the human spirit comes from the East (where the sun rises). That is the reason that Jesus Christ is called East, and the altars of our Orthodox churches are built toward the East. When we pray, we turn to the East. Our Faith is also called Eastern.

As the sun looks most beautiful at sunrise, and as it gives light and heat to the people, so Christ as a real "Sun of the Truth", came from the East, and illuminated mankind's soul and mind which were darkened by sin. He continues to illuminate them today through the Orthodox-Catholic Holy Faith.

II THE CHURCH

1. Which then is the only true Faith with salvation?

Only that One, which Christ established, which the Apostles missionized, which was taught by the Holy Fathers and the Holy Ecumenical Councils and which is taught today by His Church. That Faith is the Orthodox-Catholic or Eastern-Greek-Russian Holy Faith.

---

[3] "Соборность" - Sobornost' - this Church Slavonic word conveys a unity and a unanimity which is found throughout the Gospel. It is difficult to translate the complete meaning of this word because of its depth and ideas. The best example is the unity of God as Father, Son and Holy Spirit.

[4] * All books of the New Testament were written in Greek, not classical Greek but the spoken Alexandrian dialect called "kini" which was used and understood, by all cultured inhabitants of not only the Eastern but also the Western part of the Roman Empire at the time our Lord lived on earth. Therefore the Apostles used this language, so that all people would be able to have access to the New Testament. The Gospel by Matthew was written especially for Jews and it is assumed that it was first written in Hebrew and then probably translated by the Evangelist Matthew himself into Greek. Bishop Averky, Rukovodstvo k isucheniju Sviachennago Pisaniia, Jordanville, 1954, pp. 10-19.

[5] * Jerome the Blessed, born c. 342 at Strido, Dalmatia, and died c. 420 at Bethlehem, was the most learned of the Latin Fathers of the Church and among the greatest of Biblical scholars. He went to Syria in about 374 and spent some years among the hermits in the desert east of Antioch; there he learned Hebrew. He then went to Constantinople where he joined St. Gregory of Nazianzus. At Antioch he was ordained as a priest. From 382-85 he was a secretary to Pope St. Damasus who directed him to revise the Latin version of the New Testament. After the death of Pope Damasus he returned to the East and settled at Bethlehem. The entire Latin Bible, known since the 13 th century as the Vulgate, was either translated from Hebrew and Greek or reworked by St Jerome.

2. Are there other faiths besides the correct Orthodox Faith of Christ?
   Yes, there are many, but even though these faiths call themselves Christian, and even Catholic, they are not correct since they have not preserved unchanged the teachings of Christ the Savior. For this reason these faiths are called schismatical, heretical, etc.
3. What do the words "schism", dissidence mean?
   They mean "renegade"; such a faith or church, which has splintered off - separated itself from the Ecumenical Church in its observance of rites.
4. What does the word "heretical' mean?
   Heretical is a faith or church, which has not only reneged from the Ecumenical Church in observance of rites, but is teaching the opposite of the Church's teachings, something false or invented which is not acceptable to God.
5. Can a person please God as a member of a schismatic or heretical faith
   No, especially if he knows or hears that he belongs to a misguided faith.
6. What faiths are schismatic and heretical?
   The first one is the Papist, or as it calls itself, Roman-Catholic. The second is the Protestant, but it is divided into many parts; to the Protestants belong: a) Lutherans, b) Calvinists, c) Anglicans, d) Methodists, e) Baptists, f) Congregationalists, g) Unitarians, h) Herrnhuters, i) Quakers, j) the Salvation Army, and others. The third one is the Uniate faith, or as it is also called the "Greek-Catholic", or "Kalakuts" faith.
7. Where should we go to practice our Faith?
   To any place but most importantly to the church.
8. What is the Church?
   Church has two meanings: a) it means the people (parish), who have
   1) the right priests (clergy), through their succession from the Holy Apostles (the inheritance of the Apostles); therefore, their origin is from Jesus Christ Himself. This clergy consists of bishops (Patriarchs, Metropolitans, Archbishops), presbyters (priests, popes - pope or pappas is a Greek word and means merely father), deacons and other clergymen who were established by the Church; [6]
   2) the seven sacraments which were established by Jesus Christ Himself; these are: baptism, Chrismation, (in the Papist church there are millions of people who died without the holy sacrament of Chrismation, is that just? Our Savior did not establish this sacrament in vain), penance, communion, ordination, matrimony and extreme unction with oil;
   3) the same teaching that Jesus Christ, His Apostles, the Holy Fathers, and the Holy Councils established and gave to the Church and the acceptance of the Holy Oral Teaching as one of the sources of the Truth; and finally
   4) to acknowledge only Jesus Christ as the Head of the Church.
   b) It also means the Lord's house, the house of prayer, the house of Divine services, where Jesus Christ in the transubstantiation of bread and wine is brought as a sacrifice for us sinners to the Heavenly Father.
9. How many churches are there in the world?
   There are several: the Eastern or Greek-Russian, the Western or Latin-Roman, the Armenian, and the Coptic, but there is only one correct Christian one - the first One - the Orthodox-Catholic. All other faiths are sects; they do not have right clergy, [7] the others do not observe correct teaching and do not have all the Holy sacraments. Therefore they do not possess the Lord's Grace.
10. Why not?
    Because only this Church was founded by Christ and it is the only one that observes His Holy teaching as He commanded; only this Church fulfills everything as He said and has not stepped away from Christ and His teaching by even a hair. The other churches

---

[6] * The Church hierarchy was established by the Lord Himself; it is of Divine origin. During the time of the Apostles it became a three level organization. The hierarchy was established when seven deacons (Acts 6:5-6), then the presbyters (Acts 14:22), and the bishops were elected (Acts 20:28) and ordained.

[7] *The clergy in these organizations is without Apostolic succession and is therefore, from the canonical viewpoint of the Church, not legal.

not only stepped away from Christ Himself, and did not preserve his Faith but have even introduced sinful dogmas and customs; therefore they have become schismatic and heretical.

11. What was the first church in the world?

The one in Jerusalem.

12. Why?

Since the Church in Jerusalem was established by the Savior Jesus Christ Himself and His Apostles, the Church of Jerusalem is the mother of all churches.

13. What faith is confessed by the church in Jerusalem?

That church of Jerusalem which was established by Christ and His Apostles, confesses and preserves undamaged His True - Orthodox Faith.

14. What other churches are there?

We mentioned them above, but we will speak here only about three that concern us di rectly; those are the Papist, the Protestant and the Uniate churches.

15. When were these churches founded?

1) The Papist or Roman-Catholic church was founded in the ninth century after Christ.

2) The Protestant (Lutheran, Calvinist, and others) were founded in the 16th century after Christ.

3) The Uniate (Greek-Catholic or Kalakut's church) was founded in the 17th century after Christ. From this it can be seen that the Orthodox Church, which began at the time of Christ - can be said to be 1800 years old, - the Papist, 1000 years, the Protestant, 400 years old, the Uniate (Kalakuts') - only 246 years old. All of these churches were united 800- 900 years ago; first the Papist fell away, then the Protestant separated from the Papist and later to fool the people the Papists started the Uniate (Greek-Catholic or Kalakut faith) church. (See Remark 1 at the conclusion)

16. How did this happen?

About 800-900 years ago the Papist church was also Orthodox; it kept Christ's Faith, but the Pope and Roman bishop Nicholas I separated from the Church of Christ, and said that he, not Christ is the head of the church and that he is the successor of Christ; there- fore all the bishops have to acknowledge his supremacy.

17. Did he have the right to do that?

No!.. since the Head of the Church is only that One Who founded the Church, that is Jesus Christ Himself.

18. Can the Pope call himself Christ's successor?

No.. since it is only necessary to have a successor when someone can not do things him- self - Christ is God and He is in every place; is and will be. Christ Himself said to His Apostles before He ascended into Heaven: "Go ye therefore, and 'teach' all nations, bap- tizing them in the name of the Father, and of the Son, and of the Holy Ghost: teach- ing them to observe all things whatsover have commanded you: and, behold I am with you always, even unto the end of the world"[8] Therefore if He is with His Apostles and with their successors the bishops and with His Church, there is no necessity of a deputy to fill the office of Savior, and if someone says that there is a need, he is telling Gypsy- like lies.

19. What else do the Popes tell about themselves?

They say that they are not only the head of the Church and the deputies of Christ, but also that a Pope is infallible - which means, that the Pope says that he himself is God, since only God has no sin. The Pope says also that his position is higher than that of any bishop and king, that he is the most sacred. However as a matter of fact it happened that around the year 1000, there were some of the greatest sinners that the world has seen among the Popes; they fell away from Christ. For example: Pope Stephen VII or- dered the removal of Pope Formose from his coffin in order to bring him to trial; he then hit the deceased in the face and ordered the body thrown into the river Tiber. Pope John ordained a prist (deacon) in a stable. Pope Innocent VIII had a whole regiment of his own children. And Pope John the IX was a - woman! Pope Alexander lived with his slave Lucrecia and she bore his children. He ordained his son Caesar first as a

---

[8] St. Matthew 28 19-20

14

priest-cardinal, and then allowed him to marry! Pope Leo X was the reason that Luther separated from the Church and millions of people followed him, because the Pope started to sell indulgences. By order of the Pope there were thousands and thousands of people burned alive in Spain. (See Remark 2 in the Conclusion) Pope Pius IX blessed the Turks' weapons in 1877 when they fought the Christian Russians, who were fighting and shedding their blood for all Christians in that war. The Popes had their own army and canon; they led wars, and even went to war themselves; for example Pope Julius or Alexander. John XXIII was a pirate, robbing ships and people. Very much can be said about these Popes' "sailly" deeds but even from this very brief illustration it is clear to anyone what kind of deputies of Christ these Popes of Rom. were. [9]

20. Have the popes always been like that?

No... for eight centuries they were humble servants of our Lord and they confessed the Orthodox Faith. There were among them great man and Saints, such as St. Clement (88-97), St. Gregory the Great (590-604), St. Leo the Great (440-461), St. Pius (140-155), St. Anacletus (76-88),[10] St. Linus (67-76), and others. But after the Popes separated from Christ, they fell further and further away from God; finally, He punished them for their pride; the Italian king Victor Emmanuel took away their crown, since Christ said: "My kingdom is not of this world".[11] It must be remembered that the Italian king was also a member of the Roman Papist faith.

---

[9] * Some theologians have questioned if there is Apostolic succession of the following popes and the clergy ordained by them. The V. Reverend Peter G. Kohanik in his book _The Most Useful Knowledge for the Orthodox Russian-American Young People_ (pp. 356-357) provides a list. Joan (855) was a female Pope who gave birth to a child during a public procession. John XII, who kept a harem and "drunk to the health of the devil". John XXIII was "lewd, dissolute, a lier and addicted to almost every vice", poisoned his predecessor and is "universally looked upon as the enemy of all virtue, the mirror of infamy". He was deposed. Sixtus IV (1471) who was guilty of oppression, rape, murder, violence, and was accused of instituting brothels in Rome. Innocent VIII (1484): "Led a most profligate life". Had several illegitimate children. Alexander VI (1492): Great lover of women. Had many children. "Guilty of the blackest crimes of murder, rape, perfidy, lust and cruelty". Julius II (1503): Guilty of simony, corruption, and bribery. Wine and women were his delights. Had a daughter. Leo X (1513): "Gained the applause and esteem of the vulgar". "He was by nature addicted to idleness and pleasure, and averse, beyond measure, to all business, spending his time with jesters and buffoons". Paul III (1534): "A perfidious politician, without either faith or conscience; one wholly intent upon raising his family and ever ready to sacrifice the good of the Church to the grandeur and interest of his unnatural blood". Had one son and a daughter. Benedictus IX became Pope when he was only 2 years old. He later sold his Papal position very profitably and was married. Another example of a possible problem with the Apostolic Succession occurred after the years 1308 to 1377 when the Popes lived in France in Avignon and were obedient subjects of the French kings, supporting their policies.

Beginning in 1377, however, two sets of them tried to govern the Roman Church; the Romans elected Pope Urban VI, while the Avignon French Catholics elected Clement VII. Both sides discredited each other with curses and infamy. This period of 40 years is known in the West as the Great Schism, while the Orthodox Church considers the Popes as schismatic since July 15th, 1054. Clement VII, Benedict XIII, Alexander V and John XXIII were all antipopes during the years 1378-1415. At one time there were FOUR popes fighting for the primacy. Often popes to obtain support appointed cardinals of very sinful past and conduct. Gregory XII (1406-15) even nominated his own two nephews. The cardinals also proceeded to ordain other clergy for their own support and benefit and were electing popes. The opinion exists that through those noncanonical deeds the Apostolic Succession was lost in the Roman Catholic Church. The Roman Catholic Church has acknowledged that since the beginning of the Papacy, 8 popes were actually antipopes, exercising the Papal office in a noncanonical manner. Based on information such as that given above, Saint Alexis, Peter Kohanik, and their associates were very convincing in teaching Uniates and former Uniates about the lack of Apostolic Succession in the Roman Catholic Church. However, the Russian Orthodox Church does not share this viewpoint.

[10] *Until the reform of 1960, when the Roman Church "reviewed" the lists of Popes and Saints the Roman liturgy celebrated two popes: Anacletus and Cletus. Today only one feast is kept, St. Cletus, 26 April. It was agreed that that was the same pope under different names.

[11] St. John 18:36

21. On what do the popes base their right to civil government?
    They say that the Roman church is the first one, then they say that the first Bishop St. Apostle Peter was there, and that he was the head of all Apostles.
22. Is it true that the Roman church was the first one?
    No, we already know that the first Church was established by Christ and the Apostles in Jerusalem; that is the reason that it is the mother of all churches. The Roman church was established by those Christians who, after Christ's Ascension, left Jerusalem when the Jews began to persecute the Christians there. Then holy man such as Sts. Apostle Peter and Paul came to Rome; but they found out that there was already a parish, that is a Church, there.
23. Was Christ ever in Rome?
    As a man He never was, since He never crossed the borders of Palestine during His earthly life.
24. Was St. Apostle Peter ever in Rome?
    He was there together with St. Apostle Paul in 67 AD. He died as a martyr. But there are no records of him as the first bishop and it is difficult to prove something like that. We know that St. Peter ordained St. Clement there as the bishop for Rome, and that Clement was the third bishop of Rome. It is probable that the first bishop of Rome was St. Lin, the next was St. Anacletus. As much as is known, St. Lin, the first bishop, was ordained by both St. Peter and St. Paul.
25. Did Jesus Christ appoint St. Peter as the head of the twelve Apostles?
    There are no indications of this either in Holy Scripture, or in Holy Oral Teaching; there was no such mention even in the teaching of the Holy Fathers, or in the Ecumenical Councils. It can in no way be proved! However, everybody knows, that Christ said to His disciples: "It shall not be so among you; but whoever would be great among you must be your servant, and whoever would be first among you, must be your slave." [12] There is no word in the Holy Scripture, that Christ said to His Apostles: "Peter is the first among you, he is my Vicar, he has the greatest power among you, you have to listen and obey him". However Christ said: "All authority in heaven and on earth has been given to Me..." [13] He gave that authority to all Apostles equally, when He breathed on them, and said: "As the Father has sent Me, even so I send you.. Receive the Holy Spirit"; [14] and then Jesus Christ said: "If you forgive the sins of any, they are forgiven; if you retain the sins of any, they are retained." [15]
26. What conclusion follows therefore?
    Since it is obvious that Christ did not give to the Apostle Peter any special power, than St. Peter was not the head of the other Apostles, and he was not a bishop in Rome; [16] then the Roman bishop, the Pope is also not the head, nor the first among bishops, who all have the

---

[12] St. Matthew 20:26-27

[13] St. Matthew 28: 18-20

[14] St. John 20: 21-22

[15] St. John 20;23

[16] * The Roman Catholic Papacy claims that in 51 AD Peter had been Bishop of Rome for eight years; he continued there for a total of 25 years, and was martyred in 68 AD. The 25 years therefore commenced in 43. The following facts disprove this:- It is not stated in the Scripture that Peter was Bishop of Rome. The Roman Church was founded by the Apostle Paul. Paul tells in Gal. 1:18 that 3 years after his conversion (37 AD) he went to Jerusalem to see Peter. Peter was in prison in Jerusalem in 44 AD. In 48 AD Paul again went to Jerusalem; Peter was there in the Council. In 58 AD Paul wrote his Epistle to the Romans and sent salutations to 27 persons, but did not mentioned PETER! Therefore he was not there.
    At the end of 63 AD or early in 64 Paul arrived in Rome, visited the Christians and was visited by them. But where was Peter? He was not mentioned. In 62 or 63 Paul wrote his Epistles to Philemon, the Philippians, the Ephesians, and the Colossians but did not mentioned Peter. Paul is forsaken in Rome - "Only Luke is with me" (2 Tim 4:11). Where was Peter? Evidently not in Rome.
    Peter writes to Pontius, Galatia, Cappadocia, Asia, and Bithynia. What about Rome? Surely, if he had labored there, he would have recorded the fact - The first bishop of Rome evidently was Linus and the Apostle Peter came to Rome only to suffer the death of a martyr.

same spiritual power from Christ, being the successors and the inheritors of the Apostles. The Church of Christ, the Orthodox, honors St. Peter as the Primate, but also St. Paul; this can be seen in the fact that their holy days are celebrated on the same day; at that time in their honor we sing: "O first-enthroned of the Apostles! Teachers of the universe! Entreat the Master of all to grant peace to the world, and to our souls, great mercy!"[17] Neither the Apostle Peter himself nor the Saint Bishops of Rome thought about primacy for 800 years, but only about God's glory. Pope St. Gregory said to the Patriarch of Czargrad: "Who wants to become first among the bishops is an anti-christ."[18]

27. What do we call the power given to the Apostles with which they could release or retain the sins of people? That power is called: the power of the keys.

28. How should we understand it?
If a person sins, then the spiritual gates of the Heavenly Kingdom are closed to his soul,- but by confessing his sins, by real repentance and then by receiving absolution from the in-heritors of the Apostles (the bishops or their helpers, the priests), the gates are again open for that person's soul. Because of this, it should not be thought that St. Peter, as some people think,- received iron, or even gold keys from Christ, with which he can unlock heaven. He and also all the other Apostles received the right to give absolution or to retain the peoples' sins; he received this right as first among the Apostles because he was the first who confessed Jesus Christ as God. But we know from the Holy Scripture that St. Peter in fear, during the saving suffering of Jesus Christ, denounced Christ three times, and by so doing he lost Apostolic powers and the power of the keys. Later the Savior, because of Peter's sincere repentance, his tears and his love, declared after thrice questioning - restored, as St. Gregory the Theologian wonderfully said, restored him - into the Apostle-ship. But there was at no time any special difference between the power given to Peter and to the other Apostles. At no time did our Savior say to Peter: "You are the first among the Apostles, I am giving you a greater power than to the other Apostles" - neither did He say to the Apostles that Peter is the first among them, that they had to be under his and his successors' leadership and obey them. No, Christ said to everyone: "Receive ye the Holy Ghost" and with that He gave equal power to them all.

29. Where is the power of the "keys" kept?
St. Augustine said: Did only Peter receive the (power of the keys) and not St. John, St. Jacob and the other Apostles in the Church? No, they all received them, and that power is used everyday in the Church, when the sins of the people who repent are released.

30. What is the foundation of the Church?
It is the Faith that Jesus Christ is God, that Jesus Christ Himself is the Son of God.

31. How should it be understood?
If we do not believe that Jesus Christ is the True God, the Son of the Living God, then our entire Faith and Church has no foundation.

32. Can it be said that a person is the foundation of the Church of Christ? Not only can it not be said but you cannot even think this since the Church must be based on stable hard stone - on the Divinity of Jesus Christ, it must stand on Jesus Christ Himself, oth-erwise it will fall apart; as we can see this happening in the Papist church, which repeats that not Jesus Christ, but St. Apostle Peter, and therefore the Papacy in Rome is the foundation of the Church. Because of these teachings more and more people fall away from the Papacy, more and more religious groups are created from it by people. The Prot-estants, that is Lutherans, Calvinists, Baptists, Uniates (kalakuts), Methodists, the Salvation Army, the Adventists, all atheists have the Papist (Roman-Catholic) faith as their source; the father of all these religious faiths is the Roman Pope!

33. How do we know that the foundation of the Church is Jesus Christ Himself?
From the words of our Savior Himself, Who said to the Apostle Peter: "Blessed are

---

[17] • Troparion on the day of the Feast of Sants Peter and Paul. (A Troparion is a short hymn sung after the Little Entrance in the Divine Liturgy There is a different Troparion for each of the eight tones with special ones for each of the feasts.)

[18] St. Gregory the Great, Book 4, letter 38. See Remark 3 in the Conclusion

you, Simon.. And I tell you, you are Peter (Peter, in Greek, means rock) and on this rock I will build my church." [19]

34. How must this be understood?

These words mean: Blessed are you, Peter, since my Father Who is in heaven gave you this idea to confess Me as God's Son, and that idea, your faith is as strong as a rock... that rock is My Divinity, and on this rock - on My Divinity, on Me and on a faith, as strong as a rock, I will build My Church, a Church that the gates of the hell, (meaning the devill himself), will not be able to overpower. As can be seen in the teaching of St. Augustine, Christ is saying: "Over that stone (who is Peter),... that you have confessed (meaning Christ's Divinity), by saying; 'Thou art Christ...', then I will build My Church upon Myself, (upon the Son of the Living God- out of Myself) I will build (My Church) for you and not for Myself over you. Christ is the Foundation and also the Head of the Church, and Peter symbolizes the Church, which confesses His Divinity, and stands on Christ Himself; it is not the other way around, as the Roman church teaches.

35. Can a person have doubts in his faith?

Yes, even the Apostle Peter had doubts, when he three times renounced Christ, others also had doubts, but St. Peter cried over his wickedness and Christ forgave him, accepting him back into Apostleship.

36. Can a person be infallible?

No... only God alone can be infallible and His Church in its unanimous Ecumenical Councils with one voice, is infallible; that is when all the successors of the Apostles, all in the spirittual unity of the Faith in common consent make decisions, then the Holy Spirit speaks through them; and in that way they compose and represent the entire Church of Christ.

37. What can be concluded from all which was said above?

That 1) Christ is everywhere at every place, because He is - God, 2) that He Himself is the foundation of the Church, 3) but not the Apostle Peter, 4) that Jesus Christ gave equal power to all the Apostles, 5) therefore all bishops are successors and inheritors of the Apostles, 6) that since St. Apostle Peter was not a bishop of Rome; therefore this means that the Roman Church 'by their wickedness suppress the truth" [20] Since the Pope is not the head of the Church, nor the Vicar of Christ, nor infallible, - therefore he is only a bishop, a sinful man, who with his heretical teachings has separated millions of people from Christ and from the True Orthodox Church.

III PAPACY

1. What is the Papal teaching and what do they tell about themselves?

We already know that the popes consider themselves the head of the Church, the Vicar of Jesus Christ, infallible, the supreme Bishop, a King, a supreme Lord, who holds his position above all kings and is not dependent on anyone, does not render an account to anyone: "I do not acknowledge any civilian power nor any law..." The Catholics consider that the Pope has the highest spiritual and civilian power - in other words he is a sort of deity and is above any law. Nobody has the right to judge him. (Cardinal Manning invented this, and the Papists have already gone so far that they sinfully consider the Pope as God Himself! In their consideration the Pope comes first and then God follows. I have seen a poor Pole, and a Slovak, and I even know a ksendz - a Catholic priest - who, while speaking about God, do not remove their hats, but while speacking about the Pope, they take off their hats! This means that the Pope, in their opinion, is greater! [21])

---

[19] St. Matthew 16:17-18

[20] Romans 1:18

[21] "The Catechism of the Roman Catholic Church teaches that "Jesus Christ is the invisible Head of the Church; the Holy Father, the Pope of Rome is the visible head of the Church on earth, as the Vicar of Christ". The Orthodox Church does not agree with this teaching, considering that our Lord is with us all the time and therefore no Vicar is needed. The many differences between the Western local churches on one side and the Eastern Orthodox Churches on the other are the result of their development in different cultures. In the West

2. How did the popes destroy the faith and the Christian Church and what kind of invetions did they bring to the Church?
   From the common people the popes took the right to receive communion in both forms, the bread and the wine; the people can take the Eucharist only in the form of wafers, which have lost all appearance of bread. This is against the command of Jesus Christ Himself, Who clerly said: "Drink ye all of it, for this is My blood" [22] The Papal Church until its separation from the Orthodox Church in the 12th century, for 1200 years, gave the sacrament of Eucharist in both forms, the bread and the wine; and now it has not been done for 700 years.
3. Why?
   Because the nobility were squeamish about receiving Communion from the same chalice as the poor people.
4. What else?
   The Roman Catholics began to give the Eucharist in the form of wafers, but Jesus Christ performed this great sacrament using leavened bread. The Papist church before it saparated, up until the 12th century, (that is for 1200 years) used leavened bread and then for 700 years has used wafers.
5. What then?
   The popes forbid the ksendzes (priests) to marry; that was done by Pope Gregory VII, but Christ did not even forbid the Aposlles, and some of them were married, and the Holy Fathers also, and for 1100 years the Papal ksendzes could marry, but now for the last 800 years it is forbidden for them to do it. [23]

---

there were the differences created by the Roman pagan religion, and the Roman state organization which recognized the state ruler as a god who officiated at impressive solemn religious ceremonies. The greatness of Rome was the goal of the state and support of this goal was required from every citizen. The citizens of Rome Recognized this ideology as the source of their future well-being and security. When Rome became Christian, it dreamed of creation of a world monarchy with the Pope as the Absolute Ruler. (Rev. A. Kolesnikov, Kurs Sravnitel'nogo Bogoslovija - Course of Comparative Theology, Jordanville, 1957, pg. 7-9) This Roman ideology is the reason that the voice of the entire Ecumenical Church became the voice of only one person - the Pope. All other differences with the East were then consequences of this ideology and (ibid, pg. 12-13) the reason that the Roman Popes and their ideological followers, fearing compeltition, were intolerant of any other Christian organization that was not under the complete control of Rome. That was also the reason for the opposilion of the Roman Catholic Church to new religious, scientific, and political ideas and opinions which resulted in events and policies such as the Holy Inquisition, the Index of Prohibited Books, etc. This was also the reason for the "Holy Crusades" against other Christians in the East. That is why it was necessary to change the real miracle of Fatima into the teaching that the "Holy Virgin wishes the conversion of the Russians from the Orthodox to the Roman Catholic faith", and the maintaining even today of the so-called "Blue Army" which collects funds for the "liberation" of the Orthodox people. This is what makes Orthodox people bitter and creates suspicion about the theological and political intentions, plans and goals of the West. It creates a very distrustful atmosphere in which to attempt an Orthodox-Roman Catholic Dialog, which should in reality lead to the realization of commonality and also a unily in opposing the real threats of atheistic ideas, moral corruption and difficulty in spreading the Christian mission and helping the needy people of the world.

[22] St. Matthew 26:27-28

[23] *The family composes the fundamental cell of the Christian Church. It was established by God Himself with the creation of man and woman. (Gen.1:27-28, 2:18-24) In the New Testament the family is called a church (Rom. 16:3-4, Col. 4:15). The Orthodox Church considers marriage very important and according to the teaching of the Ecumenical Councils forbids the marriage of Christian with non-Christian; divorces are discouraged. The Church permits clergy to be celibate or married. Since the VI Ecumenical Council, it has been a rule that the bishops should be celibate or widowers. Sometime between the 4th-6th centuries, the Roman Popes insisted on the celibacy of all clergy but the Ecumenical Councils severely reprimanded that Roman praclice. (The VI Ecumenical Council in Constantinople, rule13). This resolution of the Ecumenical Council is ignored by the popes as are many others. In the year 1123, in the Lateran Council. The Papacy introduced this inhuman teaching concerning celibacy of the clergy, and in the Trident Council (1563) it was approved as an irrevocable Church law.

6. What then?

By their order and by the wish of the German King Karl the Great, they changed the Creed, adding to it the words "and from the Son" (Who proceedeth from the Father" - here they added also 'from the Son') and in that way changed the singular essence of the Holy Trinity, since the Holy Spirit now has "two beginnings". But as we know Christ said: "But when the Comforter is come, whom I will send into you from the Father, even the Spirit of truth, which proceedeth from the Father".[24] The Holy Fathers at the Second Ecumenical Council in Czargrad, and at the Sixth Ecumenical Council decided to condemn and excommunicate anyone, who would add or subtract even one word from the Symbol of the Faith, and the Pope of Rome Leo III, when the discussions were conducted, ordered that the Symbol of the Faith be inscribed in Greek and Latin on two plaques, without the addition of "and from the Son" and he ordered it put in the Roman Church, but his successors did not look at that and for the last 1000 years read the now destroyed Creed. [25]

7. And what else followed?

They have destroyed the lents, invented "purgatory" and indulgences (releases from sins), they invented the "immaculate conception of the Most Holy Virgin" and the infallibility of popes and they have also introduced Latin everywhere in the Divine services.

8. What is "purgatory"?

This is a place, somewhere in the other world, where souls are horribly tortured for smaller sins and are in a stage of waiting; the popes can release them from there, but truthfully not free of charge,- only if someone in this world will pay well for these souls!

9. Did Christ, or the Apostles, or the Councils, or the Holy Fathers teach something like that about "purgatory"?

Never; there is neither in the Holy Scripture, nor in the Holy Oral Teaching even a word about "purgatory"; nor in the teaching of the Ecumenical Councils nor of the Holy Fathers.
a) Is the belief in and the teaching about "purgatory" correct? It is not only incorrect, but it is not even Christian; it is a teaching agaist the justice and the endless kindness and mercy of God, and besides if the popes really have the right to release souls from "purgatory", then there is a great lack of mercy in the Papacy, since it releases them (the souls) only for coins, for money!.. and why not without charge?
Remark:- The Papal Church accuses the Orthodox Christian Church, Christ's Church, that it also teaches and believes in "purgatory"; that is a lie and an untruth. The Orthodox Church teaches about spiritual trials, about which the Holy Righteous Theodora and others have given us a clear understanding, and the Holy Fathers teach us (about them); and that is a big difference.

10. What are indulgences (releases)?

That is a financial (business) matter. The popes teach that for money it is possible not only to buy the souls from "purgatory", but a person can even during his life on earth buy the release of his sins from the Pope.
Remark:- Such release was, for example, granted to all "crusaders" who attacked the Christian Constantinople, robbed and killed many inhabitants there, and robbed Orthodox Churches. The Pope forgave them this deed in exchange for treasures since that was an Orthodox country. Similar releases followed for Roman clergy who led gangs which attacked Christian churches and killed people in Southern and Eastern Europe up until our time.

11. How could that be done?

The Popes teach that the saints and Holy Ones who pleased God have accomplished more of merit and did more good deeds than was neccesary for their own salvation

---

The damage to the image of all of Christianity becomes evident.

[24] St. John 15:26

[25] *The Creed was established in the Ecumenical Councils with the goal of protecting Christianity agaist heretics and the introduction of different teaching. That the Holy Spirit proceedeth from the Father alone was the teacing of St. Basil the Great, Gregory the Theologian, John Chrysos tom, Ephraem the Syrian, Cyril of Alexandria and about one thousand other Saints and Fathers of the Church who are honored by the Orthodox and Roman Churches. The change in the Creed is one of the greatest dogmatic obstacles for Eastern and Western Church unity.

and all these extra are kept in heavenly storage (on shelves), and every Papal believer can purchase them, so that his sins would be released, and even more! Such a release of sins can be bought for one day or a week, a month or even years for as long as a century! And how many souls can be bought out of "purgatory"- as many as the popes wish.

12. Is such teaching correct?

No, because it again offends the mercy and justice of God.- Neither Christ, nor the Apostles, nor the Holy Fathers, nor the Holy Councils knew about such teaching; it was completely invented by the popes in order to make way more money, and this was the main reason that there were Protestants such as Luther, Calvin and others.

a) Remark:- The Papists themselves are not fully sure and in agreement in this teaching; some of them say that a person can purchase for himself indulgence for those sins which were already committed, while other "wise" men take the position that a release can be obtained also for those sins that the person will commit in the future!... However in our opinion it is the same, one way or the other - it is not good..

b) Remark:- The word "otpust" - release, has in the Galician and Ugro-Russian dialect a meaning of pilgrimage (in Slovak it means - traveling) to the Holy places, when people go to Halich or to Pochaev, or in Hungary to Maria of Povcha, Mukachevo or other places, or they go to a parish for its patron Saint's day. There is no need to think during such a pilgrimage about a Papal indulgence, because the travel is a good deed, advised by the Lord. If someone goes to these places with faith, on foot; observes the lents, prays, observes the feasts, donates for the poor, goes for confessions and sincerely in greef presents his sins before God, then the Lord releases his sins, and there is no need to pay for this, nor to purchase the release from the Pope. The right to give such release of sins is everywhere, and can be given by a bishop or any priest. And the Most Holy Virgin, or the Holy Ones who pleased God, and to whose memory that place or church is dedicated will plead to God in the Heavenly Kingdom for the pilgrim; and not at the request of the Pope. If such a pilgrim sincerely confesses his sins, and does good deeds, then the Virgin or the Holy One does not demand money or belief in the Papacy but will for us, not for the Pope, plead to God for us in the Heavenly Kingdom.

13. What does the "immaculate" conception of the Most Pure Virgin, God's Mother, mean?

Pope Pius IX in 1858 invented a teaching about the Mother of God, that she was born without the first born (original) sin;- that means that she was born without a father like the Son of God Jesus Christ, who became a man in her womb. [26]

14. Could that be true?

No... since the Mother of God was conceived in the womb of St. Anna through her husband St. Joachim who is the father of the Most Pure Virgin Mary. St. Joachim and St. Anna - are the parents of the All-Holy Virgin Mother of God - and even though they are saints and were very religious people; they, like all other people derive from Adam and Eve and the Holy Virgin Mary also is descended from them.

15. What does that mean?

That means that every person who is descendant of Adam and Eve, even though later in life he becomes the greatest saint, still begins his life in sin and is born in sin, as

---

[26] * In 1848 Pius IX sent a message to the Patriarchs claiming the Pope's supremacy. The Patriarch of Constantinople Anfim VI in the name of all Orthodox Christians answered the Papal claim writing that a union of East and West would be possible only if the Roman Church would abolish all changes made since the 9th century. Then the Patriarch sent a memorandum to the Churches pointing out the Papist heresies. In reply, the Pope accused the Orthodox of not respecting the Holy Virgin. In 1854 he declared that hers was an immaculate conception, "By the authority of our Lord Jesus Christ, of the blessed Apostles Peter and Paul, and by our own, we proclaim the doctrine that the Most Blessed Virgin Mary, at the first moment of Conception, by special grace of God Almighty and by special privilege, for the sake of the future merits of Jesus Christ, the Savior of the human race, was preserved pure from all stain of original sin - to be a doctrine revealed by God, and therefore all the faithful are bound to profess it firmly and constantly." After this dogma was announced to the astounded Christians by the Pope, the Roman theologians began to try to justify it. It became one more obstacle to the unity of the Churches since there is no basis for the dogma in the Holy Book, the teaching of the Ecumenical Councils, or the Holy Fathers

was said by the Holy Psalm writer, prophet and Czar, David: "For behold I was conceived in iniquilies; and in sins did my mother conceive me' (Psalm 50).

16. What do we call that sin?
The sin of the first born (original).

17. What are the consequences of original sin?
That everyone who is born with original sin must die.

18. Did the Most Pure Virgin, the Mother of God, die?
That is so...Her pure soul left her most pure body as happens to every person. The only difference between her death and that of other people is that during her life she knew no other sin. She died without fear and without suffering,- it would be better to say that she fell asleep, and her holy soul was by her Son Himself, our Savior Jesus Christ carried to heaven on His divine hands. The day of Her Dormition is celebrated on August 15th. The body of the Mother of our Lord was buried for three days and then angels came who carried her body to heaven where it united again with her soul. The Orthodox Church glorifies the "Dormition of the Mother of God", while the Papal Church glorifies "the Elevation of the Mother of God to Heaven", and that way declares that she did not die, but has been taken by the angels to Heaven alive! and this teaching is wrong.

19. When and where is the person cleansed of original sin?
Every person is cleansed of original sin by the sacrament of baptism.

20. Is the sacrament of baptism necessary for salvation?
It is so important that without baptism no one can be saved, as Christ Himself said: "I say to thee, unless a man be born again of water and the Holy Ghost, he cannot enter into the kingdom of God". [27]
Remark:- The Most Holy Virgin and the Apostles were baptized by the Holy Spirit; however there is no evidence that they were not also baptized by water. It is very possible that this was so.

21. Who was conceived and born without a father as a person and therefore is without sin?
Only our Lord, God and Savior Jesus Christ. He as God is everlastingly being born from the Father-God without a mother, and as a person He was born from the Most Holy Virgin Mary, without a father, but conceived by the Holy Spirit and therefore He has no original sin. What conclusions can be made from the above? That the person who teaches that the Most Pure Virgin was conceived without sin (without original sin) is insulting the Mother of God, because when he attributes to Her this quality he creates in his mind not a person but a goddess, who would be equal to the Son of God Jesus Christ. The Orthodox Church considers such teaching as false and rejects it on the grounds that it was unknown to the Holy Fathers, the Holy Councils and cannot be found in Holy Scripture or in Holy Oral Teaching.

22. Then what is the Holy Orthodox Church teaching about the Mother of God, the Most Holy Virgin Mary?
That: a) She is the Mother of God.
b) That before, during, and after Jesus' birth, She was a Virgin.
c) That She is greater then all the angels and heavenly powers and greater than all the saints, since She is the Queen of Heaven.
d) That She is the Most Pure and Most Clear.
e) That She is the Patron and Protector of the Christian people.
f) Her glory and honor is so great in Heaven and on earth that no one on earth can add anything to it, and also no one can take it away from Her, since the Most Pure Virgin was put to such glory by God Himself. She is a comforter for the grieving and a doctor for the hopelessly ill. She is hope, She is our most kind mother. The Holy Orthodox Church, and especially the Russian people, very deeply and with such love honor the Most Holy Virgin Mary, that at every service to God, they commemorate and call on the Mother of God, and erect in Her honor the most beautiful churches. [28]

---

[27] St John 3:5

[28] *The Holy Virgin Mary has a special position and is highly venerated by the Orthodox Church. In the hymn sung at the Holy Liturgy of St John Chrysostom the Holy Virgin is described as

23. What does "infallible" mean?
    This means that he (the Pope) can't pray, make mistakes, can't gossip, tell sinful things or teach incorrectly.
24. Who can be like this?
    Only God Himself.
25. Can any person attribute such qualities to himself?
    No, and that is the reason that when the popes tell about themselves that they are infal lible they are commiting a sin, telling an untruth and a lie. By inventing these false ideas the popes bring other people into lechery and fornication because they put themselves on the same level as God. But in reality a Pope is only a sinful person.
26. Did Christ, the Apostles, the Holy Fathers, or the Holy Councils teach or write anything containing such ideas about infallibility?
    Never did Jesus Christ say to any one of the Apostles that He personally and exceptionally will be infallible, but to all Apostles and to all of His Church He said: "For where there are two or three gathered together in My name, there am I in the mids of them". [29] And then He said: "Going therefore, teach ye all nations;.. nd behold I am with you all days, even to the consummation of the world ," [30] and "But when the Paraclete cometh, whom I will send you from the Father, the Spirit of Truth, who proceedeth from the Father, He shall give testimony of Me. And you shall give testimony, because you are with Me from the beginning." [31] As is seen Christ gave infallibility to all Apostles together and to their successors; - that is the way that the Holy Fathers and the Ecumenical Councils believed and taught. [32]
27. Who are the successors of the Apostles?
    All the bishops are.
28. Do all bishops have the same spiritual power from Christ?
    Since Christ gave to all the Apostles the same spiritual power, therefore all bishops also have the same spiritual power, even that in time the Christian Church gave to some bishops, for their achivements and zeal, or for better administration, higher honors such as the titles of Patriarch, Metropolitan, Archbishop and Exarch. The giving of these titles to some bishops by the Church did not increase or decrease the other bishops' spiritual power.
29. Where was that done?
    Mostly at the Ecumenical Council meetings.
30. What are the Ecumenical Councils?
    Those are meetings of all bishops from the entire world.
31. How many Ecumenical Councils were there?
    Seven: in Nicaea - two times: the 1 st and the 7th; in Ephesus - the 3rd; in Chalcedon -

---

"more honorable than the cherubim and beyond compare more glorious than the seraphim". In services She is also called "Our All-Holy" (Panagia), Immaculate, Most Blessed And Glorified Lady, Mother of God (Theolokos) and Ever-Virgin Mary (Aeiparthenos). Her veneration was so great in the East and in Russia that every city had its own icon of the Holy Mother; many of them were miracleworking. This veneration of the Holy Virgin was transferred from the Orthodox to the Roman Catholic Church. For example when Roman Catholic Poland occupied Russian provinces, the Poles took one of the Holy Icons of the Mother of God from the Czenstochov monastery. Now it is known as the Wonderworking Ikon of the Czenstochova Mother of God in Poland. There are several other Orthodox icons that are respected by the Latin Church such as "Our Lady of Perpetual Help".

[29] St. Matthew 18:20

[30] St. Matthew 28:19-20

[31] St. John 15:26-27

[32] * In the Vatican Council, held in Rome in 1870, in the face of protests from many theologians and bishops of the Catholic Church, the doctrine of the "infallibility" of the Roman Pope in matters of the faith was proclaimed. The speech of Bishop Joseph Strossmayer in opposition to that dogma became famous. Other bishops were also against that dogma. The Orthodox Church does not accept this dogma, considering that infallibility is with the Church and not with just one person. This new Catholic dogma is also one of the obstacles to the union of Orthodox and Catholic Churches.

23

Seven: in Nicaea - two times: the 1 st and the 7th; in Ephesus - the 3rd; in Chalcedon - the 4th; and three: the 2nd, 5th and 6th in Czargrad (Constantinople) - in other words all of them were in the East.

32. Where there also other council meetings?

There were also other local meetings; when there were meetings of bishops not from the entire world, but only representing one or two countries, but of all these council meetings only the resolutions of nine are recognized by the Church as obligatory for all.

33. What should be known about the Ecumenical Councils?

That all bishops who came to the Ecumenical Council (Patriarchs, Metropolitans) represented the entire Christian Church, and all of them together made infallible decisions about what and how it is necessary to believe. Therefore their decisions begin with the following words: "It is wished by us and by the Holy Spirit", meaning that the Holy Spirit was speaking through them.

34. How many patriarchs are there?

The Holy Ecumenical Council in Chalcedon (475) established 5 patriarchates, that in honor and order are all equal; 1)The Patriarch of the Old Rome, 2) the Patriarch of the New Rome or Constantinople (Czargrad), 3) the Patriarch of Alexandria, 4) the Patriarch of Antiochia, and 5) the Patriarch of Jerusalem. But since the Roman Patriarch (of the Old Rome) or as he is called - the Pope has fallen away from the Ecumenical Church, therefore there are now only four original patriarchates - Constantinople, Alexandria, Antiochia and Jerusalem. The place of the 5th patriarchate, with the consent and permission of the other 4 patriarchs is held by the Holy Ruling All-Russian Synod with rights and privileges. [33]

35. When was infallibility invented?

It was proclaimed by the Papal church 23 years ago by order of Pope Pius IX himself in the year 1870 in Rome during the so-called Vatican Council.

36. What else did the Papacy appropriate for itself?

Royal authority. The Pope tells that he is not only Pope but that he is also a czar (king); for this reason he had soldiers and canons, led wars, condemned people to death, and had ministers and generals up until 1871. In that year the Italian king Victor Emmanuel took the city of Rome away from the Pope... and that was done according to the teaching of Christ Who said: "My kingdom is not of this world." [34] Besides none of the Apostles had any kingdom, nor soldiers, nor canons, but the Apostles like the Savior Himself were so poor that sometimes they had no place to lay their head.

37. What was the reason that the Papal power declined?

The endless pride... just imagine, how a pope is getting crowned. He sits on the main altar in the church, there where the Bloodless Sacrifice (the Sacrament of Eucharist) is brought to God the Father; - and in front of the Pope people fall to their knees, and kiss his feet - even bishops and archbishops, who have spiritual power equal to his.

---

[33] * The names of two branches of Christianity reveal their different goals. The Orthodox Church preserves and preaches the teaching of Christ, His Apostles, the Saints, the Ecumenical Councils and the Holy Fathers while the Roman Catholic Church attempts to form a universal church under the leadership of the Pope. In its preaching the Catholic Church changed the original teaching, adding new dogmas. The Orthodox Church takes as its foundation the Gospel, the interpretations made by the Saints, the Holy Fathers and the Ecumenical Councils. The Roman Catholic Church takes its information from the books of learned Roman Catholic theologians. (Rev. A. Kolesnikov, ibid p. 13-15). The Orthodox Church preserves the teaching of the Seven Ecumenical Councils. The Roman Catholic Church announces that there were many Ecumenical Councils, that an Ecumenical Council is not one where all dioceses and bishops of Christianity are represented but that "the council is Ecumenical when it is approved by the Ecumenical Bishop - the Bishop of Rome". Therefore as we understand it the viewpoint of the Latins is that even when all the bishops of Christianity meet but their decisions are not approved by the Pope, it is not an Ecumenical Council, but if there is a meeting of even three bishops and it is approved by the Pope, then it is Ecumenical. (Rev. A. Kolesnikov, ibid, pg. 15)

[34] St. John 18:36

38. What do some people say about the Papacy?
We can only state that only people who are in darkness, unenlightened; especially Poles, Slovaks and Uniates tell, that popes receive letters from Heaven; but we have to note that until now no one has ever seen such a letter.

39. Can something like that happen?
It is endless and great foolishness even to think something like that and signifies the complete spiritual darkness of people who do. What kind of truth is that, that from the sky a stone falls with a letter? - Such letters were invented by liars, who count that foolish, slow-witted and uneducated people will pay them great sums of money for all kinds of foolishness which they invent; for example: Leaves of Betjan, Stairs to Heaven, the Saturday of Mary, rosaries with indulgences, etc. This is not Christianity; and prayers with the use of such objects are not welcome by our Lord but can make Him angry.

40. How did the Papal power become so strong?
In the Middle Ages the western countries were populated by wild people. People in Italy, Germany, Spain and France did not know how to read, nor write. Those people had no understanding of Christianity, - the learning and knowledge was kept among the ksendzes (Roman clergy) who told anything they wanted about any subject. The popes did not care since they were only interested in increasing their authority. They also did not care in what way money was raised for their treasury. This was the main reason that the Popes were fooling people naive in their belief. In the East something like this could not have happened since the Greek people and their priests were very educated people.

IV PROTESTANTISM

1. What do the words "Protestant", "protestantism" mean?
"Protestare" is a Latin word; it means only "to be agaist", to speak or to teach against", - the Protestant faith therefore teaches against, speaks against some truth, namely against Christian truth and teaching; but mostly and mainly it is opposed to Papism and the Papal church and teaching.

2. When did this faith come into existence?
In the 16th century, that is 1600 years after Christ.

3. Where and who started it?
In the German country, (people) splintered away from the Papal faith.

4. Who protested?
Luther Martin.- who was a Catholic monk.

5. How did that happen?
Pope Leo X wished to build a wonderful "kostel" (church) in Rome, but there was no money to do that, so he started to write indulgences, that is to forgive people their sins in exchange for payment; many monks were sent to Western Europe and among them was Tetzel, who sold more releases from sins than others, especially in German countries. Luther opposed such "forgivers" and from the beginning he had good intentions, but the Pope and his ksendzes did not accept Luther's wise suggestions, and wanted to burn him at the stake as was done to Huss. Luther got angry and in his anger went further than he originally intended. In his accusations he started to criticize not only the faults, but also those things which were good in the Papal faith. Finally Luther established the Protestant church and faith.

6. How did Tetzel sell the indulgences?
He went from place to place, from one village to another, with a big bag and loudly shouted: "Give, give! Whoever will drop even one coin into the bag will buy one soul out of "purgatory"- and to those people who gave money he gave a card, that stated that their sins were forgiven for as long as three days, or a month or years or even for a longer time.

7. Therefore who is the main cause of the creation of Protestantism?
The Roman Pope was the main reason and only the second was Luther.

8. What happened?

Neither the Pope nor Luther wanted to give in and compromise and with each day there came also other false-teachers; more and more people accepted the teaching of Luther,- and first there disagreements, then uprisings occurred and finally a regional war came, which lasted 30 years and as a result one million one hundred thousand people were killed, the land was devastated, property worth many millions was lost, and finally the Protestants won, and all this happened because the Pope didn't want to admit his wrongdoing; to build a "kostel" with money received by selling indulgences.

9. What do we see in all that and what lesson does it teach us?

Since the Pope fell away from the true Church, he could not convince the Protestant-heretics. History teaches us that such heretical acts against the Church of Christ were committed also before Luther and possibly they were even greater; for example: those of Arius, Pelagius, Macedonius and others, but then the four patriarchs and the entire Eastern Orthodox Church helped the Western Church, or the Western Church helped the Eastern, since it was then one faith, and all that was done without war, without bloodshed, without uprisings; only at the Ecumenical Councils could the Holy Fathers stop such heretical disturbances, since the Holy Spirit himself was their help.

10. What did Luther and other Protestants teach?

In his blind anger Luther went too far, and began to preach that faith without good deeds can save a person; he rejected the Holy Oral Teaching, he rejected five Holy Sacraments, observing only Baptism and Eucharist, but at the same time he said that the bread does not become the Body of Jesus Christ, but that Jesus Christ is in bread, or with bread, or under the bread, and that is not really so, but Jesus Christ is spiritually present; he rejected the honoring of saints, and of the Mother of God; he rejected the Holy Liturgy, Holy water, Holy days, and other Holy matters. After Luther came Calvinists and Methodists, Baptists, Puritans, Herrnhuters, Swedenborgians, Unitarians and many, many other religious sects. More and more were leaving (the Papal church), and finally lost all faith... and as a result of these unfortunate Papal indulgences, now there are about 116 million Protestants! [35]

Remark: In 1844 Pope Pius IX had tried to subject the Holy Patriarchs of the Eastern-Orthodox Church to his authority sending letters to them, but the Patriarchs in their reply showed his false teaching, and indicated to him that he fights the true teaching when he introduces his own false ones and that he is in opposition to the true teaching of Christ. The Patriarchs in their reply called him the "first Protestant!" and wrote that every healthy thinking Christian will acknowledge the truth.

V UNIA

1. What does the word "unia" mean?

This is a Latin word (unio) that means union or joining; and the faith and Church that keeps such union is called the Uniate faith and the Uniate Church; or as the sensibly thinking Russian people with derision call it: the "kalakuts' faith" and "kalakuts' church".- But the kalakuts call themselves "greek-catholics".

---

[35] "As a Patriarch of Constantinople wrote, a Pope of Rome was "the first Protestant" in the Christian Church. As might be expected, the Pope's example of disobedience to the Ecumenical Church resulted in the fact that later when the dissatisfied Protestant leaders splintered from the Roman Catholic Church, they did not return to the Holy Orthodox Ecumenical Church. The reason for this of course was that while they were involved in the Roman Catholic Church, they had not learned much about Orthodoxy since the Papists were not interested in teaching about Orthodoxy, and provided incorrect information about it. Therefore these Protestant reformers were forced to depend on the individual opinions of former Catholic clergy and political leaders. That led eventually to the formation of more and more sectarian groups and the loss of most Christian dogmas, teachings and traditions, creating, as had their example in Rome, something new.

Remark: With surprise an Orthodox person who inquires in a real Russian - Uniate village, "What faith do the villagers profess?" will hear more than once the same answer "We are Orthodox Rusins.", and if the villagers would be told that they are Uniates, they will get angry and argue about that, since these poor people have not even heard about Unia! They have never been told and no one will tell them about it... They study In catechism that they are "Orthodox Christians of the Russian Faith". In church from their ksendz they also hear: "... and all of you Orthodox Christians", etc. (But in Galicia there was a plan to change the word "Orthodox" (pravoslavnyi) to "Right faith" (pravovernyi). Is that the reason that these people even today consider themselves Orthodox? The reason is also that, especially in Hungary, neither the biskups nor the ksendzes dared to announce to the people that there was Unia, that they agreed to it without the people's consent. This can be checked out by anyone who wishes to do so. Take the Slavianskii Sbornik vol. I, page 58, where it is written that: "At the Terniavskii local council our ancestors were forced by circumstances to accept Unia without the knowledge of the laity. No one has yet had the courage to say that they have committed treason to the Orthodox faith". These words were not written by some kind of "coursed schismatic"; no, they were written by a Uniate priest from Hungary - Uriel Meteor. And that is why these people also today consider themselves Orthodox.

There are three different types of Uniate ksendzes:
a) those who do not love the Latin rite, nor Orthodoxy; those are "Greek-Catholics".
b) those who are blindly behind Rome and call themselves Roman Catholics of Greek rite; most of them are in the diocese of Mukacevo, and that wonderful name was invented for them by their biskup Diula Firzak!..
c) those who in spirit and conviction are Russian Orthodox, but because of fear they are Uniates, and also because they receive their salary from the administration! If that would not be the case, they all would have left Unia a long time ago. It was also said a long time ago "naupertas est maxsima meretrix".

2. Is there such a faith and when did it start?
There is such a faith. It began in the 17th century, that is at the end of the 16th century, in the former old Poland, and in the 17th century in Hungary, Therefore it is no older than 300 years.

3. Is the Uniate faith from God?
No, as the people invented the Papal and Lutheran, so also was the Uniate faith invented by them.

4. Who invented this faith?
Two godless persons, sellers of Christ, - two Judases, the Bishops Cirill Terletzky of Vladimir-Volyn' diocese and Hipatius Potzey of Lutzk. With sorrow it must be said that they were leading Orthodox bishops, but already from the beginning of their careers, they led lives mean and unfit for clergy. Terletzky was married twice and led a depraved life. Potzey was born an Orthodox Christian, then he became a Calvinist, then a follower of Papism, then again Orthodox and died a Uniate.

5. Why did they do a thing like that?
For benefits; partially for money, but mostly they were afraid of early retirement, which especially was a threat for Terletzky as punishment for his unworthy life, - since his Holiness Patriarch Jeremias intended to demote him from a bishop to a monk.

6. What benefits were promised to them by the Roman-Catholics?
They were promised the same rights in the kingdom of Poland, as the Polish bishops had, that they would become Polish senators, and even advisers of the Polish king. But all promises were never fulfilled since the Polish nobility and ksendzes (clergy) could not re spect traitors to their own Church and people. [36]

---

[36] Bishops Potzey and Terletzky fraudently obtained the signatures of Gedeon Balaban, Bishop of Lvov, and Michael Kapisliansky, Bishop of Peremysl, on a clean sheet of paper, on which they claimed they were going to write a petition to the Polish king in support of privileges for the Orthodox Church in Poland. Instead, they wrote on this paper, as if in name of a synod, a request to the king and the Pope for a religious union of the Orthodox Church in Poland with the Roman, on the terms of the Council of Florence, with the conserva tion of all the discipline and ceremonies of the Orthodox Church. In 1596 the Orthodox clergy assembled in Brest

7. Who belongs to the Uniate church?

At the present time there are about three and a half million Russians in Galicia, one half million in Hungary, about 400 thousand Romanians in Hungary, and some Bulgarians, Greeks, Arabs and Chaldeans in Europe and Asia, but their number is not greater than 6-7 million. Before there were more of them.

8. Why was Unia invented for these nations?

To convert them little by little into Papism and to make Latins out of them. Unia is only a bridge for these people on the road to Latinism.

9. How did Unia begin?

The countries Lithuania, the Ukraine, Little-Russia, Volynia, and Galicia are today under the strong and powerful guidance of the Orthodox Russian Emperor; some of them are partially inside the borders of Austria, but these are completely Russian lands. Before they were occupied by the Polish king and were part of that kingdom, they confessed the true Christ's Orthodox faith. But the Poles who are blind followers and supporters of the Roman Popes began to oppress the Russians who lived in their kingdom, planning to destroy them; from the start the ksendzes and Jesuits attacked the faith and the Church with the intention of making Latins out of the Russians. But the Russian people, their bishops, priests and nobility did not even wish to hear of such a plan. Then the ksendzes and Jesuits invented Unia: but the people didn't want even then to join it until the Jesuits attracted Terletzky and Potzey.

10. What does Unia consist of?

The Jesuits and ksendzes expected only one thing from the Russians; that they would accept the Pope, not Christ as the head of the Church; and it was promised that they could keep all other traditions, rituals, and language. They planned that as soon as the Russians were subject to the Pope, the other things would be easier to introduce. What happened? When Terletzky and Potzey, those two Judases, were bribed, they went to Rome. There on their knees they kissed the Pope's feet, promising loyalty. In doing this they committed treason to Christ and to the Church, and also to the Russian nation. As soon as that happened the Polish ksendzes started to act differently - first they started to attract the Russian landowners (nobility) to Unia. The Polish kings began to promise them advantages. Some of these people joined Unia and later became zealous Papists and Latins. The same happened to the Uniate bishops. The Polish Papists acted as Uniate Bishops and introduced Latin customs and rites into Orthodox churches such as whispering the liturgy and the use of organs and bells. They introduced special matins and vespers and destroyed the entire cycle of yearly services to God. Then they took the iconostasis out of the churches and destroyed the lents. Then the Uniate ksendzes accepted the Papal vestments, began to shave, and even to shave the tops of their heads; even worse they started to persecute unmercifully the Orthodox Faith and Church. But people stood firmly for Christ, for His Faith and teaching, and accepted for that tortures and death. They went to prison and suffered but did not denounce Christ.

11. How were the Orthodox people treated by the Papists and Uniates?

Those people who were not afraid of torture and threats were instead made all kinds of promises; this did not work and consequently the people were treated severely.

a) Their Holy, Only Saving, Christian Faith and Church were called "peasant".

b) Their priests were called "jews" and under the leadership of Polish ksendzes or Jesuits the priests were attacked, beaten, even dragged on the ground by their hair and beards.

c) Corpses were thrown from their coffins. During funerals the dead and the mourning parishioners were dragged to the marshes or to waste places. The priests and Orthodox believers were hit and many times people were even killed.

d) The Orthodox churches, it is horrible to say, were turned over to the Jews to control. When an Orthodox priest needed to have a service, to baptize or wed or bury people

---

and divided. Some joined the Roman jurisdiction, but a majority decided to stay loyal to Orthodoxy and be as before under the jurisdiction of the Patriarch of Constantinople. Since that time two Churches have existed in Poland and Lithuania, one called Orthodox and the other Uniate; each had its own succession of metropolitans.

he had first to pay money to receive the key and to be admitted to the church. [37]

e) On the Holy Day of Pascha if an Orthodox person wished to have a blessed kulich, [38] he had to buy it from the Jew; if he baked the kulich himself, then he had to buy an approved seal for it. Without that Jewish seal the kulich was not allowed to be blessed. If priests did it they were punished by a jail sentence.

f) More than once a gang gathered under the leadership of a Polish or a Uniate ksendz and for "fun" they attacked the poor Orthodox people, sometimes during the Divine service, demanding that the Orthodox people accept Unia; and if the parishioners did not agree, the gang locked the church and set fire to it, so that all the faithful would be burned!..- The greatest torturer was Josaphat Kuntzevich, a Uniate archbishop of Polotsk, who went from place to place with his servants and supporters. He tortured the priests and faithful Orthodox people, killed, took away or burned some of their churches until he was killed himself. And this villain, do-nothing, dirt and bandit was declared a Catholic saint by the Pope of Rome in 1858; that gangster was called a "hieromartyr". It was ordered that the Uniates should pray to him in their Divine services, honoring him as a saint, which the Uniates did. As we see the sufferings of the Russian people were unspeakable, they were persecuted; books can be written about all of their sufferings in Poland from the ksendzes and the Jesuits; and all because they were being forced to accept Unia and then the Latin rite.

12. How did Unia end in Poland?

When the Papists were on their uncontrolled rampage, then the patience of God came to an end. The merciful Lord heard the cry of His people and the poor Russians obtained mercy and Poland was punished, since Austria, Prussia and Russia divided Poland and some of the Russian regions were reunited under the protective, strong, fatherly and benign hand of the Orthodox Russian Czar. The poor people happily swept away the spiritual yoke - the sickening plague of Unia and as result finally millions were reunited with the Church of Christ. They returned to the Orthodox Church together with their bishops, priests, with their churches. Only several thousands of Russians, who became completely Polonized, and who were called "kalakuts" by the Russians stayed Uniate! But Poland was lost. It disappeared forever. It was wiped from among the nations for its sins. In the same way that God punished the Jewish nation He also punished the Poles, since they also persecuted Christ and His Orthodox Church! The remnants of the plague, Unia, are still found in Galicia and in Hungary.

13. How did Unia influence the Russian people?

Most cruelly, since the Uniates began to shame their Church and even their nation and became Polacks.

14. When did Unia start in Hungary and why?

It started in Hungary in 1649. The Orthodox people were persecuted there by the wild Hungarian-Papists, who persecuted them as did the Poles in Poland. They used the same methods as the Poles: beating up people and promising all kinds of benefits, and finally under such pressure 70 ksendzes joined Unia in the city of Ungvar (Uzhorod).

---

[37] *The Jewish minority in Poland was used first by the Poles, then by the Russians for collecting funds. When the Russian troops returned to Poland after the Napoleonic Wars, one of the leaders of the Cossack Army, D. Davydov, wrote in his memoirs that he entered the city of Grodno and was well received by the local Jews and their leadership. The Jews of the city happily met the Russians and Davydov declared to the Polish population that the government of the city had changed. The police functions in the city would be carried out by the Jewish religious organization headed by a Jewish chif of police, who had to be informed about secret meetings and other activities. The Jews gave Davydov the lists of Poles who supported the Polish government. D. Davydov, Sochinenija, 611 pp. No. 1962, pg. 398-399 The local Jews were already familiar with using the Russian administration to fight their own religious dissidents, who according to them were spies, troublemakers and not dependable. (For example see Kabbalah, Library of Jewish Knowledge, N.Y.- Israel, 1974, pg. 287-309, Jacob Frank and the Frankists). The Jews asked the Catholic and Orthodox Churches for help to combat these "unbelievers" and asked even the local government for military assistance.

[38] *Kulich- for Paskha (Easter) the Russian Orthodox faithful prepare specially baked bread, (special cheese with sweets, colored eggs and other food) and put it in a basket to be blessed after the Church Service

For one hundred years people who would not join the Papists were jailed and tortured and persecuted. They were forced to denounce their grandfathers' Orthodox Church; and not only their faith and Church, but also their nationality. Therefore a major part of these people became known as Slovaks and Hungarians! These people were so much influenced that they were ashamed even to say a Russian word and became the same kind of kalakuts as those who lived in the old Poland. [39] (See Remark 4 at the conclusion)

15. What kind of future is there for kalakuts (Uniates) today in Galicia and in Hungary?

A very disturbing one. In Galicia they are becoming Polonized, - and in Hungary they are continuously persecuted by the Roman-Catholic ksendzes and monks, who constantly visit the homes of Russian people forcing them into the Latin Rite. They build Roman-Catholic kostels (churches) in Russian villages and at the same time hold the Uniates up to ridiculousness. The Poles appointed as Uniate clergy unfit men such as Silvester Sembratovich, who already held the opinion that the Uniates received too many benefits from the Latins. Under the influence of the Papacy and the Poles, he wanted to introduce the practice of clerical celibacy and new holidays commemorating the Body of Christ, the Immaculate Conception of the Holy Virgin, the some persons by the names of Torquemada and Arbuesis, who burned people as did also the villain Josaphat Kuntzevich. He closed the Russian seminaries in the cities of Lvov and Vedni by order of the Pope and the Polacks, and thereafter the Russian priests had to study in Roman-Catholic Jesuit seminaries. All this was done to bring the people completely under the authority of the Pope and to transfer them to the Latin Rite, to make Poles out of Russian Galicians. These priests did not care about their Russian flock; they left their villages in Galicia, the Russian Church and Nation. They thought only about Polish favors and the Pope's kindness; for those they gave away the Russian monasteries to the Catholic Jesuits. Now he (Sembratovich) also planned to bring Jesuits into the seminaries but was awarded with what he earned, as he returned from his trip to Rome. Youth at the Vedni railroad station, loyal to their Russian Faith and Nation, threw rotten eggs at him. They accused him of going to kiss the Pope's feet and of selling out the Russian people as did Judas, and 300 years ago, Terletzky and Potzey.

16. Therefore what kind of future can be forecast for the Ugro-Russian kalakuts (Uniates)?

It is not better. They are Magyarized; in schools they are not allowed to study Russian. The children are being taken from their families; they are put on exhibit for ridicule and those who speak Russian are prosecuted. The bishops select and keep only the clergy who like money, who are interested in titles and in feeding their stomachs. They send the Russian clergy to study in Catholic seminaries under the pretense that they do not know how to serve well. Neither these bishops nor ksendzes speak Russian among themselves. Such unfits as Pankovich, Pastelij of Ungvar (Uzhorod), and Toth [40] and Valyi, bishops of Presov diocese, do not love the people. They think only about favors and kindness from the Pope and the Hungarians; they bow their heads to them. The Hungarian Papists and the Poles in Galicia tell kind words to their faces; behind their backs they laugh. They do not respect them or the poor Russian people and call them "stupid rusnaks". This is the reason that these poor people are uneducated, are ashamed of their own past, and are attracted to something foreign. To avoid all this persecution, the population of some entire villages left and moved to Russia or to America. It is not a miracle! They must suffer when they are laughed at, are persecuted, are hungry and cold and all of that only because their bishops and ksendzes do not stand up for their protection.

17. Where then does Unia stand as a faith?

Nowhere... It is neither Roman, since it keeps Orthodox Church Rite, even though it is now distorted, nor is Unia Orthodox since Uniates do not consider Christ but the Pope as

[39] In everyone's memory is still the Turzansk comedy, when an entire village changed into the Latin rite, and how many Turzansks are there in Galicia and in Hungary?

[40] * According to St. Alexis, his uncle, the Bishop of Priashev, played cards. Once he lost, and to make the payment sold the silver chalice from his cathedral to an antique dealer, who happened to be Jewish. As St. Alexis, before comming to America, bought back the chalice, which had been a gift from the Russian Czar Alexis to the Orthodox principality of Moldavia. He brought it to St. Mary Church in Minneapolis

the head of the Church. In other words it is something funny; neither a fish nor a lobster. [41]

18. How do those who belong to the Uniate faith call themselves?

They call themselves "Greek-Catholics", meaning that they are Greek-Catholic - but in reality they do not have any right to call themselves that, since they are Uniates or kalakuts; and the Uniate or kalakuts' faith is invented by people as are the Papist or Lutheran or the Salvation Army.

19. What are the Uniate churches and Divine Services like?

In many places the churches are built facing toward the west. Inside there are statues made of wood. They have added several altars in the church. There are glorifications to the bishops, supplications; they have introduced Latin rite holidays, the iconostasis is no longer built in the Uniate churches, the matins are not served anymore, nor vespers nor the Proskomide as is done in the Orthodox Church. In many places during the Divine Services, the ectenia (litany) is left out. Sometimes the priests serve the Holy Liturgy by whispering it. During the services they use little bells. There are such things as rosaries of "Jesus' Heart", then they introduced holidays of the "Body of Jesus" and other holidays like that. The Uniate ksendzes often can be seen during confession wearing Papist vestments that they use even during the Divine Service, (especially every day in the School of St. Augustine in Vedni); but it must also be observed that the Papal Uniate ksendzes (Roman Catholic priests assigned to Uniate parishes) wear Orthodox vestments. In Italy the Greek-Uniates perform the liturgy without the use of Prosphora but using wafers. In Galicia the Proskomide is completely left out or they serve only the ninth hour instead of the vespers. They chant the akathists, and during the liturgy glorify the bishops. They bring out the statues for religious processions and carry them. They use bells (for bringing the Presanctified gifts to a sick person). In many places there is no shroud of Christ, instead there is a figure of Christ made of wood. In other words there is much that is left out and much which is foreign has been added.

20. Why was that done?

To be closer to the Papists, to convert Russians more quickly into Latinism. This is the reason that the Uniates are continuously told that: "the Roman and the Greek faith are the same" - and people believe that, especially in Hungary, and until now thousands have already changed their faith and their Russian nationality...

21. And what are their bishops and ksendzes doing?

There is only a small number of those who love the Russian faith and nationality, since they are under persecution by other bishops and by the government, and the loyal people are being called "Moskaly". The bishops now fulfill the obligation of police people for the government. They do not protect their flock and are interested only in how to increase their own profits. They do not speak Russian in Hungary. They and their ksendzes speak among themselves either Latin or Hungarian. They dress and shave like the Papists and feel proud doing that.

22. How do the Roman-Catholic biskups and ksendzes treat them?

In front of them they are very nice and polite to them, but behind their backs they laugh at them, and even though they say that "the Roman and Greek faiths are the same' - why then do the Papists never go to the Uniate churches? The Uniates go to theirs! The Roman-Catholics are very happy, when they get into the Latin rite even one Uniate who will denounce his faith and nationality, and become a Roman-Catholic; this means more to them than if 10 Protestants would become Catholic. You have to know, that the Papists are the extreme enemies of Orthodoxy, and the Uniates even greater. The Uniates have the greater sin, since they would exhibit their own mother to mockery!.. Both of them do it for one reason: the Orthodox Church every day makes their falsehood obvious, and puts their wrongdoings right in front of their noses. It is known that "the home truths are hard to swallow"... that is the reason that the Uniate ksendzes would rather permit the Uniates go to a Protestant church or to a Jewish synagogue, than to permit them to go to an Orthodox Church, since there peoples' eyes might be opened.

---

[41]* A Russian expression equivalent to the English expression, "neither fish nor fowl".

23. What do the Papists and Uniates say about the Orthodox Church?
In their rage and stupidity they tell all kinds of fables, but mostly they tell: a) that Orthodoxy is a "Muscovite faith", b) that the head of that faith is the Russian, or as they say "Moskow's" Czar, but at the same time they tell: c) that that faith does not have any kind of a head; and d) that the Orthodox people do not respect the Mother of God.
24. Is all that the truth?
All these accusations are obvious stupid gypsy-like lies, every word of them is rubbish, since:
1. There is no such faith as "Moscovite". There is no such nationality either on this planet. There is a great, glorious, mighty Russian nation and the Uniates are brothers of that nation. The Hungarians and the Poles are the greatest enemies of the Russian people; they assume that the Uniate people are in spiritual darkness and they tell them that they are not related to the Russians... The word "Moskal'" (Moscovite) was invented by Poles and Hungarians and the Uniate ksendzes repeat that nonsense and by doing that they fool people who come under their jurisdiction. Since the Great-Russian nation confesses the Orthodox faith it also became known as "Russian", and as we know the Uniates call themselves Russians (Rusins)? They call also their church and faith Russian (even though that is not the truth since they are Uniates, kalakuts):
2. The Russian Czar (Emperor) is a Russian, and not a "Moscow's" Czar; his title is "Sovereign" and Emperor (Caesar) of "All-Russia"; which means of all the Russians on this planet. He is not any kind of head of a church, as the Pope is. He does not give orders how and what people should believe. Isn't that true? Or not? He never does anything of that kind; but the opposite. He obeys the Church laws and the commandments of Jesus Christ, in the same way as his poorest citizens do. The Russian Emperors are a good example for their people of obedience to the Christian commandments; the Russian Czar is the first son of the Holy Mother Church, and of the Orthodox faith. He preserves and protects the Church of Christ. Millions of rubles and rivers of the blood of his citizens were offered for the faith and Christ and His Church. The Russian Czar and his brave champions have liberated the Russians from the Polish yoke; they liberated the Serbians, Greeks, Romanians, Bulgarians - from the vile Turks' yoke. Each true Russian - even if he is not the Czar's citizen, every person, who has even one drop of Slavic blood - has to pray for his health and for his royal house, because the Russians and the Slavs have in the Russian Czar their only protector on this planet. If the bishops are elected in the name of the Russian Czar, this does not mean that he is the head of the Church. That is how it is done in Austria, Italy, Spain and many other Roman-Catholic countries, that the rulers of these places (kings) are selecting or appointing bishops. If they do not do that, does it also make all of them heads of the Roman-Catholic Church? Besides, it must be said that the Russian citizens do not kiss the feet of their Czar; especially bishops and priests do not do so as is done in the West by Papists to the Pope. He (the Czar) does not sell indulgences, and does not teach anything about "purgatory". But the Russian Czar kisses the hand of a bishop and even of a priest at the Church service (while receiving a blessing or at the veneration of the cross etc.). He also goes to confession and observes the feasts as a good Christian should do.
3. They (Papists and Uniates) tell that the Orthodox Church does not have a head, as they do have - a Pope! Isn't the Church the living body of Jesus Christ? Doesn't the Orthodox Church continue to live and work to save the souls of the faithful? Doesn't it spread the teaching every day? If the Orthodox Church did not have a head, could it operate like this? Can anyone live without a head? For 400 years the Orthodox Church in the East has existed under the vile Turkish yoke; it is still not liberated but it lives and works. Can there be found on this planet another country where there lives another such religious, faithful and Godfearing nation as the Russian? Where there are built such beautiful, great and wonderful churches, monasteries and schools? Where there are as many Holy Ones who pleased [42] * God as there are in Russia. There are in Russia so many

---

[42] * Holy Ones Who pleased God are people who according to the Orthodox Church led righteous lives on earth and now are in Heaven with God. They pray to the Lord for us, helping us who still live here on earth.

miraclemaking icons. Where has the Mother of our Lord shown so much mercy and love through miracles as in the East and in Russia? Didn't God make Russia so mighty for its strong belief in the Orthodox Faith? Therefore a person who talks idly about Orthodoxy doesn't have a head himself.

4) The Mother of God and the Saints are highly venerated by the Orthodox Church; we already spoke about this before.- We will finish by saying that only hatred, stupidity, darkness and spiritual blindness can speak about a "Moskovite" faith, about the idea that the Czar is the head of the Church or about the headlessness of the Orthodox Church, or that there is no veneration of the Mother of God; a person who tells something like that should be sent to a mental asylum.

25. And who is then the head of the Orthodox Church?
Jesus Christ Himself, the Savior of the world, our God, Who has established the Orthodox Church; He is the only Head and He is the only One who rules the Church through the Holy Spirit.

26. Who administers the Orthodox Church on the earth?
The successors of the Apostles - the Bishops, Metropolitans, Patriarchs and the Holy Ruling Synod. The Church of Christ is divided by nations, but united in faith and in teaching; not divided. There are Russian, Greek, Serbian, Rumanian, Arabic, Syrian, and Chaldean churches, but the pastors of these churches are under the guidance of Jesus Christ Himself, and live according to instructions from the Holy Ecumenical Councils, by the teaching of the Apostles and the Holy Fathers and by the Holy Oral Teaching. In other words they act according to the Holy Spirit.

27. Who rules the Russian Orthodox Church?
The Holy Ruling All-Russian Synod.

28. What is that?
This is a meeting of Fathers and Archpastors (Bishops and Metropolitans), blessed with God's wisdom, 12 in number, more or less - who work for the wellbeing of God's Churches; not only for Russian churches but also for others.

29. What kind of spiritual power does the Holy Synod have?
Power equal to the patriarchal - it is equivalent to each patriarch and exists by agreement with the four Eastern Holy Patriarchs; having been established in place of Moscow's Patriarch - and therefore the Holy Synod was established by God's providence in place of the Roman patriarch who is now called the Pope and who has fallen away from Christ and His Church.

30. In what part of the world does the Synod exercise its authority?
Over the Russian Church in Europe, Asia, America and Australia.

REMARKS

1. When we start to speak of the unfortunate "Unia", then the Papists, and especially their cringing Uniates, who would like to become better Catholics than the Pope himself, like to straight off refer to the "Ecumenical" (?!) Council at Florence. What they are trying to prove (?) is that "Holy Unia" is much older than 300 or 246 years, that "Unia" was accepted not only by the Russians but also by the Greeks, and that the "Unia" of Old Poland existed since 1695 and the "Unia" of Uzhorod since 1649. This "Unia" is based on the results of the "Ecumenical" Council at Florence. To be able to speak about that "Ecumenical" Council we must know what kind of qualities there must be for it to be called an Ecumenical Council. It is necessary:

a) that the bishops would come to the Council not for civil advantages, but with a spiritual goal, in the name of Christ and for the protection of the true teaching of the Orthodox Church.

b) that the delegates would come to the Council also in the name of Christ, with conviction, that the Holy Spirit is invisibly present there, that there would be freedom of debate, brotherly love and unanimity.

c) that the resolutions of the Council would be accepted by all Churches, even though some of them were not represented by their bishops at that Council. (The 2nd Ecumenical and 1st Czargrad Councils had only representatives from the Eastern bishops, but the whole Church of Christ has accepted their resolutions and teaching).

But if at the Church Ecumenical Council there is talk about earthly matters, benefits, and goals, if there is no free speech, and when the bishops' delegates are controlled or forced to make certain decisions, then such a council is far away from its name of ecumenical. The Church of Christ strongly denounces such mistakes that were made for example at the Council at Ephesus by the Bishop of Alexandria, Dioskur; or at the so-called "Ecumenical" Council at Trident which was held by the Papists, who insist that that "Council" was more important than all Councils that were held by the Holy Fathers. At that "council" there was fighting, they pulled each other's beards and really proved what kind of shepherds they were when each one tried to prove his truth. Also at another "Ecumenical" Vatican Council in our time, what kind of "freedom" (?) was exercised there; 764 Bishops came to the "Council", 163 of them left Rome for all kinds of reasons. The most important one was not to make Pope Pius IX angry, and to save one's own conscience, since he blindly believed in his own "infallibility". Eighty-one Bishops did not take part in the vote, 91 abstained, 51 voted with "conditions", 85 voted against "infallibility", and only 283 bishops blindly accepted the teaching of the "infallibility" of the Pope! Of those 283 bishops, two-thirds were Italians, who were supported by the Pope's treasury in Rome during the event of a concil! Therefore they had to dance according to the tune, that was given by the Pope! It is a myth that later all bishops "agreed" to accept the infallibility of the Pope; that is simply a comedy! since they knew, that the Pope would not play games with them... but simply would relieve them of their bishoprics, and that would be difficult for them, especially in some countries to leave the bishop's throne; when the income was in thousands, and no work had to be done, only to be a lord, as for example in Austria, Hungary, Italy, etc. With this in mind, look at the "Ecumenical" Council (?!) in Florence:

a) Did they come in the name of our Lord Christ and for the protection of the teaching of the Orthodox Church? No! There was a different goal: the Greek Emperor (Caesar) wished to purchase help from the Pope and Western Europe against the Turks, who threatened his kingdom. And at the same time, the Pope in every way wished to fulfill the hope of every Pope since Nicholas I: for the Papacy to subjugate the East and the Eastern Orthodox Church. At the same time the Popes feared the authority of the decisions made by the Council at Basel which the Popes accepted as the highest court even above themselves. Therefore as we can see the name of Jesus Christ was used only as cover for civil conquest at that "Council".

b) Were any free discussions conducted at the "Council" and were they sincere?

No - not at all! The Greek Emperor influenced and forced bishops from his country to agree with the demands of the Pope. The Pope who took over all the expenses of the Eastern Greek bishops for the entire length of the "Council", gave the necessary support in such small quantity, that the Greek bishops had great difficulty all around. They were kept hungry with the intention that they would accept more quickly the teaching of the Roman Church. At last there was no brotherly love left among them. There falsehood and anger dominated the "Council" - the Greeks wished to give up less, and the Papists to receive more. At the Papal divine service, the Greeks took part, but didn't wish to receive a wafer for communion, and during the ceremony of brotherly kissing, the Greeks kissed only Greeks and the Papists only Papists. The Greeks wished to have a service of their own, and wanted the Pope with his bishops to take part in it but the Pope did not allow that to happen!.. Looking at all these facts, who will then say that he is convinced that the invisible head of the Church, Jesus Christ was present there at the "Council"? That it was led by the Holy Spirit? And finally what happened when under pressure from the Emperor and the Pope the decree about Unia was signed?.. Pope Eugene asked if Saint Mark, Bishop of Ephesus (who was the successor of the Apostle and evangelist John) signed the decree acknowledging Unia? When he received the reply "No", then he said: "then the entire Council and work were in vain"... because even though other bishops were forced to sign that agreement about Unia, Mark, Bishop of Ephesus was not afraid and firmly stood for Christ and His Orthodox teaching! When the Greek bishops returned home, and their faithful found out that they had committed treason to the faith, they became angry and at the local Councils of Czargrad and Jerusalem, the agreement made at Florence acknowledging Unia was rejected and the bishops that took part at that "Council" were forced to leave their bishoprics and were confined

34

in monasteries for the rest of their lives, to mourn their treason to the Orthodox Church! The voice of the people, it is said, is the eye of God, and that was exactly what happened in that case. The same was done to the traitor Metropolitan of Moscow Isidor. When he returned home to Russia, and began to declare the Pope as the head of the Church, then the Russian Czar and people and the entire Russian Church chased him from Russia! He went to Rome, where he stayed with the Greek Cardinal Bissarion!

Those were the results of that "Ecumenical" Council of Florence, and what happened later. It should be shameful to Uniate-kalakuts to make references to that "Council", since it brought for them only as much use, as did the Old Poland and Uzhorod Unias, that is: it created a new faith and a new slavery for people.

2. The Spanish Inquisition was an ecclesiastical court, where Dominican monks judged everyone, using horrible tortures, if someone made even a little remark against the Papal church or the faith or the Pope himself or his bishops. Every court decision ended with a death sentence on a poor person who was burned alive! That Inquisition was established by Papal order and thousands of people were burned. The main villain inquisitors were Peter Arbuesis and Thomas Torquemada. These were shouted out as saints by the Pope as also was the kalakut Josaphat Kuntzevich! God protect us from that type of saint. Whoever does not believe us should take the service book, the Lvov edition, and there in the Proskomide can find that after Sts. Basil, John, Nicholas, and Aphanasius is written also: "St. Holy Martyr Josaphat".

3. About the fact of the presence or absence of St. Apostle Peter in Rome, much was already said and written, especially during recent times; even in 1872 there was a public discussion about that subject in Rome. It ended with the Papist declaration that: "Even if St. Peter was in Rome only one day, that would be enough for us", and when they made that statement, it became clear to others that they themselves did not believe without reservation that St. Peter was there for 25 years as a bishop. There is also a Latin saying about the Pope: "non videbis annos Petri" (you will not see the year of Peter), which means that none of the Popes will rule more than 25 years and therefore it becomes a joke, since Pius IX was Pope for 33 years! About these subjects the author of this work has written another with the title: "Was St. Apostle Peter in Rome?"

4. The Uniate ecclesiastical seminaries in Hungary are in the cities of Ungvar (Uzhorod) and Presov, but they both teach according to the Papist tradition; all subjects in the seminary are taught in Latin or Hungarian, the Latin orders hang on the walls, there is also a picture of the Pope in every corner. When a biskup, rector, or any administrator arrives at the seminary, they speak either in Latin or Magyar! Six-eight years ago in the Uniate seminaries there was the triumphant memorial celebration of cardinal and "saint" Charles Borromeo. [43] But what good did that "great saint" do for the Uniates? They themselves do not know that!.. The clergy, being educated in Budapest or in Ostrigome in Latin rite seminaries, knows very well that the knowledge of how to perform the Presanctified liturgy does not open the world to them! They do not know even how to read good in Church-Slavonic. The deceased Archpriest Kustodiev was present at one Divine service in a Uniate cathedral. As

---

[43] * Charles Borromeo (1538-84) was related to the Medici family. At the age of 22, he received a doctoral degree. His uncle Cardinal de Medici became Pope Pius IV, and appointed Charles to the position of cardinal and gave him important appointments. He supported his uncle at the "Council" of Trent, in decisions and the drawing up of a new catechism for Roman Catholicism, helped write edicts which permitted the printing of the Talmud, which stopped the deportation of Jews from Bohemia and which stopped the persecution of non-Catholics. In 1583 he was appointed to Switzerland to deal there with witchcraft and the teachings of Calvin and Zwingli. He died at the age of 46 and his very wealthy family created a cult around him. In 1610 he was canonized by the Roman Catholic Church. Some theologians oppose the methods that were used in obtaining that type of canonization.

35

he heard a "deacon" read the Gospel, he thought that the reading was in Hungarian! That "deacon" was a graduate of Budapest! And how many such "deacons" are there!

4. Recently a "prayerbook" appeared (for members of the "Living Rosary"). It was translated by Alexander Mykita but composed by a titular canon and "Doctor of Divinity" from Ungvar (Uzhorod). This gentleman probably doesn't have any idea that there are in the Eastern Church Akathists, [44] thanksgiving services, and other special services! And therefore the dear Uniate-kalakut ksendzes are surprised and defamed; the Russian people in Galicia and Hungary can more easily converted from their Eastern rite to the Latin! But what can be expected of the people if such "luminaries" and "Doctors of Divinity" themselves are guiding their people to foreign beliefs? to some kind of "Rosaries", and "Akathists" instead of vespers. This practice was introduced and only God knows what else they teach? The Latin proverb:"Contrarii iucsta se rosila maeluses cunt" has never expressed such great truth as it did in last issue of the newspaper Kelet, 1 51 of 1893. The newspaper is supported by the Hungarian government and printed for the Hungarized Ugro-Russians. In the article "Prudentia pastoralis" one ksendz complains that the Latin ksendzes are trapping Uniate-kalakuts into the Latin rite! The following article, written by another Uniate ksendz - "The American Greek-Catholic Vicariat" in the same publication is a song accompanied by guitar music. With a calf's delight [45] there was printed a lengthy glorification to the Papal delegate Satolli for his agreement to all demands of Uniate-kalakuts(?). He reports that now there is "a Vicar" and married clergy can freely come to North-America(!?), that all rights of the "Greek-Catholic-kalakuts church" have been recognized as they were.(!?) In other words in heaven it is no different, there are only bass singers and the psalters players are hanging around! In general it must be said that nothing controls the kalakuts' fantasy... but that someone would believe such naiveties and even put them down on paper. The self-deception which for some time has occupied the lives of the Uniates must be very important to them! They are beaten and persecuted; their Uniate church and their church rite is displayed for mockery by the Latin rite, and they submit even more obediently to them. Satolli or his kind of person will tell them something pleasant or a kind word and they become delirious and are happy, because their hidden enemy was kind and merciful to them. Such selfdeceiving naivete brought them much harm... but what more? They trusted, they will look to their enemies for salvation... To trust a slave - that's the nicest music!

5. The Papists like to say very often, and the kalakuts to repeat, that the Holy All-Russian Synod always makes its decrees by order of his Imperial Majesty. Evidently they are ready to say,- that this means that the Czar is the head of the Church, since the Synod gives its decrees by his order. True! But why is that done as it is? The Papist-kalakut fantasy is already to weak to answer that question... they cannot understand it. It is very important that the resolutions of the Synod would have not only Church but also civilian power!... But when making these accusations, these people forget that the Austrian Emperor and Hungarian king gives his credentials to the appointment of biskups and clergy. Sometimes he tells to ordain someone else. The German Emperor, the Spanish king and also others do that. Those accusers know it well because in these countries or in Italy, if the king or Emperor does not give his agreement to the appointment of one or another biskup, the Pope can appoint him one hundred times and give his special blessings and offer him indulgences for one hundred years for free,- but still if the king will not appoint the biskup, or will not give his agreement, then the Papal appointment is not worth a cup of water or a sniff of tobacco!.. besides the ksendzes of that region will also not accept that biskup!... Therefore where is it done better? - In Russia, or in other places?

---

[44] *Akathist is a service that consists of many hymns of praise to the Savior, the Holy Virgin Mary or some Saint. It is sung in church or at home. The word Akathist is from the Greek meaning "not to sit".

[45] "To "come into a calf's delight" is a Russian expression which likens the bouncing behavior of a calf in a pasture to a person who loses his mind about something and under the influence of that delight loses sight of reality.

CONCLUSION

The entire world was surprised by the friendly and great reception of the Russian ships by France in October of 1893. And really that was a great and glorious deed. We are not dealing with politics; we will talk only about the church festivities since Catholic France is "the first daughter of the Catholic Church", and it was in kostels glorifying God, that the "schismatic" Russian ships accepted the Frensh invitation. In Paris the Archbiskup Cardinal Richard served a "Te Deum", and what kind of letters did the Frensh Catholic ksendzes write to the Russian "schismatic" priests? We will talk here only about two of them:

1. The cleric of the Arass diocese, dean of the kostel of St. Nicholas in Boulogne, wrote the following letter to the presbyter o f the (Russian) Royal clergy Fr. Janyshev:

".. Permit a Catholic priest to express to you all the happiness, that the Frensh clergy experienced on the occasion of the visit made to France by the Russian squadron." "I can speak naturally only for myself, in the name of a Frensh priest, who belongs to his jurisdiction,- and in the name of the parishioners, who were entrusted to my pastoral care, but I also know the mood of the Frensh cardinals, archbishops, bishops and priests and therefore I can state to you, that in all of our hearts is imprinted deep love for Russia, for His Majesty Alexander III and for His Royal family. France, the real France, is deeply impregnated with Christianity and she prayed from the depth of her soul for Russia. We, the Frensh priests, would like to reach our friendly hand to the Russian priests: aren't we brothers in Christ our Lord Jesus? Isn't our priesthood the same? Don't we confess the same faith in almost all details? Don't we venerate in the same way the Most Holy Virgin?

If Your Reverence, by any chance would come to France, I, the signatory of this letter would be honored to receive you and show you how great are our friendly feelings for Russia and how great is our love for our brothers, the members of the Russian clergy.

Would Your Reverence let the people surrounding you know about our feelings, and tell them that Russia can count on us to stand together for life and death..."

"I have the honor to call myself Your Reverence's most humble servant Shouke, cleric, pastor of the church of St. Nicholas in Boulogne."

2. The Bishop of Nimes, Monsignor Zhilli, sent to the clergy of his diocese a circular letter, where he states, that the festivities all around France on the occasion of the visit of the Russian squadron are caused by the fact that the two nations can be a guarantee for future peace. In conclusion the Bishop said: "The examples of religiousness shown to us by the Russian sailors must remind us that in necessily our Lord as He always has, protects the army. All kingdoms depend upon Him. When He wishes, He will give to the nation great signs. We have witnessed as these sailors from their wonderful ships, in their churches in Toulon and Paris turned to Him with their prayers and sang "Te Deum". And we in our turn have to thank God for the great mercy sent to us, and therefore tomorrow, on the Day of All Saints, we have to serve from our hearts thanksgiving services". (Listok, 1 23, 1893, Ungvar)

What will the kalakuts and Papisls, who still repeat that "schismatic Moskals do not believe in the Holy Trinity", that they "do not venerate the Lord's Mother" and other things tell to that? And how can the Lord's "heir" and the "most holy ecumenical Pope" Pius IX himself explain his blessing of the Turkish army to conduct war against the Christian Russians? Pope Leo XIII did not know what to do in his happiness, that those "Moskals" and "schismatics", in reality the great and mighty glorious God-fearing Russian people, and their Sovereign Emperor, crowned by God's will, reached their hand in friendship to the Frensh people!... And (the Pope) showed them his affection and mercy!...

Therefore we can conclude that the Pope also thinks more of Russian friendliness and Russian glory than about his own infallibility.

HOW JESUS CHRIST LIVED
AND WHAT HE ATE WHEN HE LIVED ON EARTH, AND HOW HIS ALLEGED "VICAR" (?) - THE POPE OF ROME IS LIVING AND WHAT HE EATS.

Our Saviour Jesus Christ as a man during His earthly life was humble until His death; in His conversation and preaching Grace came like honey from His mouth,- even when He was punishing and severely reproaching. - He was however shoving love to mankind, that which He was always doing, according to His words, fulfilling "the wish of the heavenly Father" and He was also teaching people, that they would do the same. His eating was always modest,- vegetables, bread, honey, fish that was His food, during Pascha according to the law of Moses He ate lamb and He drank a little bit of wine, but mostly He fasted and constantly He stayed in prayer,- He honored the leadership and taught the people to fulfill the law. He told them "Render therefore to Caesar the things that are Caesar's and to God the things that are God's," [46] and then "every authority comes from God"; to Pilate He said that, "You would have no power.., unless it had been given you from above"- [47] He forbid the use of weapons- "Put your sword back into its place" [48] He said to Peter, He taught "love one another". [49] "Love your enemies", [50] "Judge not and you will not be judged", [51] those seeking Him He accepted with love - even the greatest sinners for example an adulteress,- the robbers on the cross,- if He was going from one place to another, then He did it on foot,- only once in His life He sat on a foal and only to show the Pharisees, that He was a king and His descent was from the House of David; He was angry only then when He saw, that the House of the Lord - the Temple of Jerusalem - was turned into a house of trade,- as a man He had no shelter! The Saviour said "the Son of man has nowhere to lay His head." [52] He taught His disciples, that they would not swear "either by heaven, or by the earth..." [53] He taught that they would be humble,- and He showed it by examples, since He washed their feet,- He taught that they would not care about earthly goods- and He did not give them any authority other than spiritual, He told them "My kingdom is not of this world" [54] and even that He was by birth from a king's house the only crown that He wore was a thorny one,- but He carried a heavy cross on His shoulders! To the people rigorously repenting and believing in Him, He forgave sins without charge! Finally for His friends - for people - He gave His life, and sacrificed himself to God the Father... This was Jesus Christ - the son of Abraham, Isaac, Jacob, and David, as a man, He lived on the earth when He established there His Church, of which He is Himself the cornerstone and the base, and to which He is Himself the head forever, since He said "I am with you always to the close of the age"!.. [55]

Now look, how that one lives who calls himself "Head of the Church" and "Vicar of Christ", "Infallible Teacher", who holds himself as "the first in church"! That is - the Pope of Rome...

---

[46] St. Matthew 22:21

[47] St. John 19:11

[48] St. Matthew 26:52

[49] St. John 15:12

[50] St. Luke 6:27

[51] St. Luke 6.37

[52] St. Matthew 8:20

[53] St. Matthew 5:34

[54] St. John 18 36

[55] St. Matthew 28:20

The cardinals will elect him, they who do not have any right to do this, since neither Christ, nor apostles and Holy Fathers, Seven Ecumenical Councils, and generally the entire Church of Christ knows anything about cardinals... Then they crown him - at the coronation put a tiara on him, a valuable triple crown! (You remember - that Christ wore a thorny garland!) and then they set him on the same altar, where the bloodless sacrifice is made! He is carried on the sedan chair (sedes gestatorin) on peoples' shoulders, and the Swiss guard with swords and halberds surrounds him (Christ walked on His feet!); it used to be before that the cannons were firing, and the soldiers were standing around with their weapons when the Pope was dragged to the kostel, - (Christ was congratulated by Jewish children who stood with branches and sang "Hosanna to the Son of David!" [56] Instead of apostles the Pope is surrounded by princes, crown princes, dukes, and Roman gentry, who are fabricated by him, the Papacy doesn't sheath the sword, but orders people killed, for example: John Huss, Savonarola, Bruno, - by the Pope's order in France thousands of people were killed in one night (St. Bartholomew night) and to glorify this killing the Papacy held a service in Rome (there was some kind of a service to God?),- by the order of Pope Innocent III, villains-crusaders were hanging, burning, killing in the East hundreds and hundreds of people, priests, bishops, and they were Orthodox; they burned Orthodox churches, they robbed them; Pope Urban VIII sent an order to the Polish king, that he should kill his Russian subjects, if they did not want to accept Unia "do not spare Peter's sword" wrote Pope Urban! (and Christ told "Love one another! Love your enemies!") The Pope has his own kingdom, soldiers, cannon, weapons,- they have been leading the wars, and the Popes have been taking part themselves in battles (Alexander VI, Julian II) (and Christ was telling: "My kingdom is not of this world"!).

The Pope is proud, with a belly out as a frog and he was damning, anathematizing the kings and the common people, and how he did it! For a soldier, or a Hussar it would not be appropriate to use such language! (Christ taught: "Do not swear at all neither by heaven.. or by the earth..."!) The Pope blessed (what kind of a blessing could that be?) the yataghans, the bayonets, of the Turks who were slaughtering the Christians,- now he blessed the Spaniards who are killing the poor Cubans! The Papacy does not acknowledge any authority, and will not obey any law said Cardinal Manning, and the Popes have put down kings, and emperors and he stepped over their necks, when he mounted a horse.- he encouraged subjects to rebel, and not obey their kings (and Christ taught: "Render to Caesar what is Caesar's" and also that "Every authority is from God"). For money the Popes absolved the sins of people and kept souls in "purgatory" and did not let them out of there, if the indulgences for them were not paid (Christ told that for repentance and faith: "Your sins are absolved", but he was not selling indulgences!).

The Pope lives in a splendid king's palace in the Vatican which has 11,000 rooms- (Christ did not have a place to lay His head!). But even that is not enough for him: he calls himself a "prisoner" (and the holy apostle Peter, whose successor the Pope wants to be also was a prisoner, but he was sitting in prison, and not in a palace with 11,000 rooms!). When in 1848 a revolution started in Rome the Pope did not remain there, but was the first one to run away dressed as a coachman, and also other times, when there was danger, popes tried to save their "infallible skins"! Eugene, Felix, Pius VI, Pius VII, Pius VIII, Pius IX, and Gregory VII and others also (Christ gave his life for his friends!). As it was said above, Christ fasted more than ate, and when He was eating, it was very frugal,- the Pope is "gorging" four times a day and he is "guzzling" wine, we can read what he eats:

What Pope Leo Eats
At 8 A. M.
Oranges
Rolls.   Coffee with hot milk, or Chocolate.

At 11 A.M.
Eggs, poached.   Omelette, with fine herbs.

---

[56] St Matthew 21:9

39

White Wine.	Squab, broiled.
Red Wine.	String Beans.
	Green Salad.

Cheese.

At 4 P. M.
Bread, cut thin and buttered, and honey.

At 6:30 P. M.
Oysters on half shell

Glass of Sherry.	Consomme with spring vegetables.
White and Red Wine.	Boiled Fish.

Potatoes sprinkled with parsley and freshly melted butter.

Poulard, steamed.	Fresh String Beans.

Macaroni, plain.

Leg of Mutton, roasted.	Turnips, mashed.
Salad, with stewed Fruits.	Plain Rice Pudding.

Sponge Cace.

Glass of Madeira.	Fruits.

Coffee.

Before retiring.
A glass of Mulled Chianti with Dry Biscuit or a light Water.

So it was reported by the English newspaper "World" of June 8, 1897.- As it is seen from above the Pope is gorging himself on coffee, milk, chicken meat, calf, lamb, rolls, sauce, eggs, omelette, chocolate, fish, oysters, salad, macaroni, potatoes,- and mainly he "sucks" fife times a day, white, red wine, even Madeira, sherry, and chianti wine, except this he also does not forget one "for a sleep"!...[57]

It seems, that it is not so bad, and that "the prisoner of the Vatican" is not really living in any poverty! Many poor people would like to live in such poverty as this "prisoner"!...

Now let's compare, how lived Jesus Christ the founder of the Church of which He is the head,- and how were and are living those "pans", who tell that they are "Vicars"- deputies of God on earth, the Pope of Rome.- I know, that the loyal sons "of the Holy Father" will ask, are the other successors of the apostles living as the apostles did? Certainly not completely, but however they are living in a more humble way, more poorly, than the Pope, they do not forget the fact, that they are sinful people, they are fasting and they are praying, and the most important is they do not claim for themselves God's characteristics,- they are God's servants, but not gods, as the Pope claims to be, and the fools believe him, and they are teaching it, that the Papacy is the third incarnation of Jesus Christ - that was done by Bellarmine, Barony, and in our time it shattered the biskup of Rouen;- if the Popes of Rome want to be gods, then they have to live "godly", and then they should not show at each step human weaknesses!

---

[57] All items on the menu mentioned by Father Toth were given in the Russian diminutive form.

FROM THE HISTORY OF THE ORTHODOX CHURCH IN **WILKES-BARRE**

In the last days of November, 1892 - I received a letter in Minneapolis, Minnesota from the curators of the church, (in Wilkes-Barre - Ed.) in which they called on me to accept the leadership of the parish in Wilkes-Barre, and I have to admit that this surprised me very much! What is Wilkes-Barre?- The future cathedra of the future Uniate biscup?... I thought, that this was either a joke, or some kind of misunderstanding; because of that I wrote a long letter (on 11 double pages!) to the curators: what is the Orthodox faith, what is the Uniate, asking them if they know, what they are doing? What is the reason for such action on their part? To this I received a reply by telegraph: "We know all of that,- but come as soon as you can".

What could I do?... In spite of the terrible distance (very far) 1200 miles I went there and arrived on December 3rd new style in Wilkes-Barre,- but I did not go to the parish house but to the Hotel Wyoming. As soon as one curator Michael Jevcsak learned about that, he came there, and involuntarily I had to leave the hotel and move to the parish house! Even though this was Saturday, the parish house was filled with people, and I clearly made explanations about everything: what it means to unite with the Orthodox Church; - they were all satisfied, and namely they like, that finaly they will have a bishop.

The next day the 4th of December during the service after the Gospel, I to considerably many gathered people, explained clearly in their native language, what is - Unia, when and where it started, what kind of harm and what disaster it brought, for the Galician and Russian people in Hungary, how the Russian people were persecuted, how they were tortured, how the jerk and villain "Hieromartyr" Josaphat Kuntzevich set fire to the churches, and killed people and for this the Papacy made him "a saint"; then, what is Orthodoxy? What does it teach? that only the Orthodox-Russian Church and faith can call itself redeeming, since it was preached and spread with Christ, by His Apostles and the Holy Councils, and by the Holy Fathers: I shoved that, the supremacy of the Pope, his infallibility is a human invention; that he spoiled the symbol of the Creed [58] (I believe..), that the Roman teaching of "immaculate conception of the Holy Virgin" [59] - all this opposed the teaching of Christ and the Church,

---

[58] * The Western Churches did not preserve the Creed as it was formulated by the Councils of Nicea and Constantinople where it was decided to use the exact words of the Holy Scripture, adding nothing to the expression "who proceedeth from the Father" in the conviction that nothing thought of by human mind must be added to that revealed by God. Roman Catholics have added to the Creed the words "and from the Son", in Latin "Filioque". This addition was made in Spain in the 7th century. It spread under the influence of Emperor Charles the Great and Rome admitted it only in the 11th century at the request of Emperor Henry I. When in the 16th century the Anglican and the Protes tant Churches undertook to correct the abuses of the Roman Church, they did not oppose this addition. This arose the East- West difference in the Nicean Creed.

[59] * In the year 1854, Pope Pius IX published a bull: "By the authority of our Lord Jesus Christ, of the blessed Apostles Peter and Paul and by our own, we proclaim the doctrine that the Most Blessed Virgin Mary, at the first moment of conception by special grace of God Almighty and by special priviledge, for the sake of the, future merits of Jesus Christ, the Savior of the human race, was preserved pure from all stain of original sin - to be a doctrine revealed by God, and therefore all the faithful are bound to profess it firmly and constantly." The Orthodox Church believes that this Catholic dogma does not have foundation either in Holy Scripture, or in the Holy Tradition of the Christian Church and teaches that the Most Holy Virgin was born according to a promise but still of man and woman both. For only the Lord God Jesus Christ was born of the Most Holy Virgin Mary and of no man, but, in a manner ineffable and inscrutable, of the Holy Ghost This dogmatic difference made possible the accusation of Orthodox people during the mission of Father Alexis by Uniates and Catholics that "Muscovites" do not believe in the Holy Virgin.

that "indulgences" are foolishness [60] and have been invented, to fill the Pope's pockets, and so on; only the sermon continued for more than an hour and a half! After that I called them, if they give up and are ready to renounce all this Uniate foolishness, and to believe in that which the Orthodox Church and faith teaches, than I will accept the church from them. And to let them have enough time to think about this and to talk it over, I am giving them a full three days, and only then, that is on the 6th of December in the evening, I would like to hear their decision. After the service all curators came to the parish house,- and it was told to them, that they would go to all places where there are living people belonging to the church and would ask them the following:
1) Do you want to unite with the Orthodox Church and faith?...
2) Are you agreed, that the church, the parish house and the cemetery would be given over to the Russian Orthodox Bishop, who lives in San Francisco, Cal.?
3) Do you renounce the tie to the Uniate-Papist faith?

If all these points will be answered clearly, with determination, then let each sign his name, or put the sign of the cross on his name on the paper which was given to every curator, and which is confirmed by the church seal; - it is severely prohibited under oath to talk people into it or to say anything else; it was also instructed not to ask for signatures from Roman Catholics and Protestants, since the church is only a Uniate one, and the Catholics are not considered to be its parishioners!... On the same evening there was again a crowd of people in the parish house, and all were talking happily, that "finally thee is going to be order"... and they asked first one, then another about Unia, about Orthodoxy - and even more than one of them admitted, that they already from their soul pastors, that "that faith, which we have now (Unia), is not the right faith: it is only forced upon us"...

Until late night I led the discussion with them, and in the morning about 7 o'clock I went to Hazleton, and from there to Shenandoah and I returned only on Tuesday afternoon.-- In the evening about 7 o'clock the parish house started to fill with people; the entire house, the yard and the basement of the church were full of people, there were present all the curators and the lawyer Mc-Aniff. To all people gathered once more I explained shortly about Unia, and about Orthodoxy, and finally I asked them, do they wish to unite and to save themselves in the Orthodox faith, do they wish to give all the church property to the Orthodox Bishop in San Francisco to subordinate themselves under his spiritual rule?... all unanimously answered: "We wish!"... Then the petition to the Orthodox Bishop in San Francisco was read, to the Most Reverend Nicholas, in the Little-Russian language, which Michael Jevcsak explained in the Slovak language... To my question "Did everyone understand everything? they loudly answered: "We understood!" "Do you give the church, and everything else to the Orthodox Bishop of your own will, freely without force?" The answer was "We give!". Then I took out a watch and word for word said, "Now it is 8 o'clock. I give you 15 minutes more, and if only one person be found who will protest giving up the church then I will agree and will depart from you, without demanding anything for my expenses, which are more than $80, and the matter will remain as if we never talked!... And there was silence: it can be said - not one word was heard... I went to another room...

After 15 or 20 minutes passed I returned, and again I asked, "Do you want to give the church? Are you uniting with the Orthodox faith? Are you going to subordinate to the Orthodox Bishop... Did you think it over well?- "We thought and we wish it so"... was the unanimous answer. "Then sign the petition and the statement about this" - I told them, and all curators, as the representatives of the church, two presidents of the fraternities - namely: Saint Peter and Paul, and John the Baptist, signed it, and then put the church and fraternity seals on these documents: and the key of the church, as the sign of the surrender, was given into my hands by the head curator Andrei Pivowarnick with the words: "I give to you

---

[60] * The Roman Church teaches that, the souls of such dead as have not received absolution from their sins on earth, or have received absolution, but have not undergone any temporary punishment, go to Purgatory of which there is no mention made in the Holy Scriptures Therefore the Orthodox Church declared that if sinners could be cleansed of their sins by suffering, there would have been no need for the Son of God to be made incarnate and to suffer They believe that at the last judgment, God will Himself decide the future of the souls and therefore no one. except Him can give absolution to the dead

our church and its property freely, by my own will and with the agreement of the entire parish"!...

The signed petition, and the statement with all the signatures, collected by the curators, which on that evening were 400, and by the next Sunday there were more than 600, were sent by me to San Francisco, and on the 12th of December I left for Minneapolis, Minnesota.

By the request of the people of Wilkes-Barre, by the blessing of the Bishop I remained in Wilkes-Barre during the holidays of the Nativity of Christ, Epiphany, and, seeing that, the church had neither iconostasis and had not been built right: its altar was to the west, [61] and there was no Oblation Table on it [62] - and instead of the Oblation Table there was a washstand, after long conferences with the curators, decided to rebuild the church, so that it would as much as possible look like a Russian Church; I showed the plans of the church and nobody said a word against it, there has been agreement and peace among the people, and the blessing of the church was done on the 29th of June, 1893 by the Most Reverend Bishop Nicholas in the best order. The Russian seamen which at that time arrived from New York, were met by the parishioners received and treated with zeal... and this didn't give any peace to the enemies of Orthodoxy - to the stubborn Uniate ksendzes, - especially because at the same time as the people in Wilkes-Barre, the Uniates in Pittsburgh, Allegheny, and Osceola started to move for unity with Orthodoxy: this frightened the ksendzes and they started to counsel among themselves, but they couldn't find a reason to seize uponl... they ran around Washington, around Baltimore, by the Papal delegate, along the Cardinal and along the biskup' entrance halls, and assured them, that the "schism" threatens to swallow "Unia!"... But what can be done? According to reliable reports it was decided first, that they will make a report to our Federal Government, that the "schismatics"- horrible to say! in their churches are praying for the Russian Czar!... and they forget, that they are not in Austria but that they live on free American soil, and that here with such fears there cannot be put "fear to the Liakhs" [63] and that nobody can be proven committing "hochverrat".[64] Nothing can be proven and they would only make them-selves look silly.

THE HOLIDAY OF CHRIST'S NATIVITY VS. CHRISTMAS

What is the difference, - the reader will ask, - both mean the same thing, the only difference is that one is the Russian expression and the other is in the English?...

Indeed so and still there is a difference between the Holiday of Christ's Nativity and the American "Christmas".

Look into the calendar for the past year, 1904. Christmas is always celebrated on December 25th and in this year we also see Christmas marked on December 26th. This means that the Americans in this year were celebrating for two days instead of the usual one. So what happened here?

---

[61] *In all Orthodox Christian churches, the sanctuaries look to the East, the area of the world where Christ appeared

[62] *The Oblation Table is placed against the wall on the left side of the sanctuary There stand vessels and other objects that are an integral part of the Liturgy. It is here that the elements to be used in the Divine Liturgy for the Holy Eucharist are prepared before the beginning of the service. During the procession of the Great Entrance, these Holy Gifts are brought from the Oblation Table to the Holy Table

[63] *Liakhs - Poles

[64] *Hochverrat - High treason (German)

43

In the entire Christian world, or at least in the larger part of it, the Holiday of Christ's Nativity is celebrated on December 25th, the Incarnation of God's son is celebrated on this day. In other words, it is a purely religious holiday. But in America, correctly in the United States, it is not like that...

In the entire world this holiday is celebrated by Christians,- the unbaptized have no connection with this day because this day is the day of the birth of Christ, the Redeemer of the world. In America it is celebrated by everybody and at least one third of the population does not know and does not want to know that (Christ - Ed.) "rose upon the world as the Light of Knowledge", [65] there are many who are counted as Christians in name only, they are bowing to the "stars" without learning anything from the "Star". Because of this, American Christmas is some kind of a mixed celebration and it is celebrated not only by Christians but also by Jews and other unbaptized!...

In the United States, as a visible expression of the celebration of Christmas or as a symbol of it is some kind of monstrosity called Santa Claus,- appearing as a grey-bearded old man, in red pants, short coat with a papakha [66] on his head, in boots... sometimes he drives a sleigh with four or five deer, full o all kinds of presents for children, and he pours those presents through the stove chimney into the children's stockings which are hung for this purpose in the evening in almost all the houses, where there are children who expect presents for the holiday. Already a few weeks before Christmas, Santa Claus appears in the streets in his impressive costume and loiters along, sometimes dragging on his back advertisements and labels of some unChristian company: "Come to us, it's cheaper"!... and sometimes he sits in the shop windows of the same companies and with his grimaces attracts the public into the store. Who and what this Santa Claus is, is difficult to comprehend. If you ask an American - he will only answer that Santa Claus is Santa Claus, and that's it! In all probability it may be strange, but this Santa Claus is nobody else but the distorted personality of obedient St. Nicholas, gracious protector of children... How did they arrive at this, that this saint was converted into an old man who drives deer and throws presents into children's stockings, possibly no one can explain. And there is no way that an American would study the exalted character of St. Nicholas!... He is occupied with "business"! And nobody should be surprised by this because even a Slovak who acts like a priest in America turned once to me with such an astonishing question; - I quote him word for word "Why do you Russians so highly respect St. Nicholas? He was such a simple man who could not even write"... What then can we ask of the Americans? They have as much relation to St. Nicholas as we to the North Pole.

Another form of expression of Christmas is the fir tree,- which is decorated vividly in many colors, - but you will see this fir tree not only in Christian houses, but also in those of Jews who want to appear in the role of "high toned" liberals! And in their houses little Sams and Ikes (Samuels and Issacs) are jumping around the fir tree and admiring the presents which Santa Claus brought them!... Also Christmas is expressed in an obligation to send or to give presents to relatives, friends, servants and to all acquaintances and this pleasant tradition has been brought to such a state, that some Americans await with horror the coming of Christmas, when they voluntarily or involuntarily will be forced to play the role of Santa Claus. There are such people who shamelessly demand presents on Christmas. If you do not give them, that is the end of friendship.

Concerning the spiritual side of this holiday, a distinction should be made between Roman Catholics and Protestants. Roman Catholics priests, in the morning at six o'clock whisper the first mass which is called the missa pastorum! (Probably al that time the shepherds in Bethlehem had already heard the mass!...) They whisper the second mass at eight o'clock. And at ten o'clock they perform the high mass with singing and tambourines, drums, violins. Every priest has to perform three masses on this day.

In the Protestant churches, there is no night service on this day; simply in the morning and evening an extensive musical program is performed, one which is publicizes in advance in the newspapers to attract people. Naturally the programs are mostly composed of

[65] "From the hymn and collect of the Nativity of Christ

[66] "A tall Caucasus hat usually made of sheepskin.

vocal religious music but sometimes you will find included Mendelssohn's Wedding March, the marsh from Lohengrin, by Wagner, etc. Then naturally there are sermons about everything but not about Who was born and Whose day is being celebrated! It seems that Christmas is a celebration which can be appropriately celebrated by everybody,- Christian and Jew, Chinese and Negro, baptized and unbaptized.

In the year 1904, the celebration was extended to the day of December 26th because by the law of the United States on Sundays, as also on Election Day the taverns are closed and how could such a festive day as Christmas be celebrated with closed taverns? On Sunday there should be no work and Christmas should be a celebration, so why then should a day free from work be lost, therefore, if not only Christmas but also another holiday which is acknowledged by the state, for example, New Year's, Fourth of July, and others fall on Sunday, then the celebration is carried over to Monday. So the New Year of 1905, the Happy New Year, was celebrated by Americans not only on the first but also on the second of January... So as it should be, to enjoy the celebration well and worldly...
That's how Yankees celebrate their Christmas.

ROMA LOCUTA - COMEDIA FINITA

Anyone who knows what kind of politics is conducted in Galicia in relation to the Uniates and then knows under what conditions S. Sembratovich was elevated to the Metropolitan's see and later became Cardinal, can, with complete certainty, say that in the future the "provincial" Council of Lvov will not treat the Galician Russian people fairly; that all resolutions of that Council will only enslave the Greek-Uniates more to the Latin and Jesuit propaganda, and in that way what has not been accomplished or was forgotten by the Uniale of Brest, Cardinal Sembratovich will try to fulfill!...

Today the resolutions of that Council are already known to everyone since the Pope has approved them and "pro striclissima observantia" has sent them to the unfortunate Galicia for publication.

It had long been expected: finally, the "Congregatio de Propaganda Fide and Synodiuum" examined those arrangements; maybe in Rome this time occurred a very rare happening, - when the matter concerned the Eastern Church and the Eastern Rite:- the conscience awakened, even though it is very risky to assume so... In any case it so happened that both congregations decided, and Summus Pontifex approved it: Cardinal Sembratovich and his satellite can now rejoice,- and it remains for the Russian people of Galicia with the nation's faithful representatives and the majority of clergy to sob and cry! That which is happening over there now - is something different, the "beginning of the end!" Papism and Polish Jesuitism have won,- and if in some way God's providence will not help the Galician-Russian people in today's misfortune, then in two or three decades Russian people in Hungary will become extinct and become Polish!...

Until now Rome and Jesuit-Polish propaganda at least hid their nasty and cunning goals: the Infallible Shoewearer and inheritor of pagan Roman Pontifex Maximus - the Pope - had always proclaimed from the time of Urban VIII until today's diplomat Leo the VIII, that "Rome honors the Greek Rite", that the "Popes do not want to make the Easterners Latin, but only - good faith Catholics". But tempora mutantur, and now the Jesuit-Papal propaganda does not find a reason to make secret its goals, but manifestly says, that the Pope has approved the resolution of the Council in Lvov mainly to bring the Uniates to the Latin Church! This is the first frank and outspoken word of Rome to the Easterners!

What will the Uniates do now?... Naturally, I have in mind only those, who have not sunk completely in the Papal swamp, who still have some feelings, and who sometimes think: namely - the Uniates here in America!.. The Galician-Russian priests today refer to the fact, that they are only legally, subject to Cardinal Sembratovich.- Consequently the

45

parishes here in America are "partem integrantem" of the Lvov diocese, and therefore they have to introduce also here "hours", "the Body of Lord", "Holy Days", "the Reincarnation Feast", "the Religious Society of the Holy Virgin"; the newspaper "Katolik" published a long list of things that have to be introduced in the churches here, among them "rosaries", "prayers in the month of May" and other things. Then they would call those "Risen from the dead", the "Dominicans", the "Capucins", and the "Jesuits" to come on the mission and most importantly they would have to have the churℎ vestments in 5 colors "for the benefit of the Latin Church!" As for celibacy, it is already de facto introduced in America by the Cardinal, since the local Galician Russian priests are all widowers or single,- and since they also do not have beards, it would be very easy for them to establish by means "of other ways unity with the Apostolic capitol", since morally that is what is expected of them!...

Up until now we did not read anything in "Svoboda" about what and how "the patriot ukrainophils" are planning?- In my sincere opinion, they should have talked about that, and not only occupied themselves with burble about "peasant movements" and fill up the columns about "frankists" foolishness, by twisting the history of the Russian people; writing topical satires for example about the canonization of Taras Shevchenko, exhibiting his photographic or painted portrait in church during the Divine and vigil services. [67] That is really surprising! - "Svoboda" cries about the fate of "38 million Little-Russian people", whose fate is in excellent condition in all respects, who are ruled by the Sovereign of the same faith, who respect him - and to whom they are loyal and honorable; these people do not know anything and will not ever know about their self-proclaimed "guardians". "Svoboda" mumbles about "slavery" and "persecution" of the Little-Russian people in Russia... in other words about something that doesn't exist. But about what happens at their home,- that in Galicia the faith, nationality, rite and language are being taken away from the Russian people,- that they are being polonized, that they ran away across the ocean; about all of that "Svoboda" does not want to hear at all!... All that they are interested in is - "Polish-Socialist people's movements" there is no word for it; to collect money for "peoples movements", to fool themselves and the poor people!... Is that the "enlightenment of people!?...

Now there is a question: are the decisions made by the "Lvov council" acceptable to the Ugro-Uniate dioceses? Naturally they will be, through per analogiam. The Ugro-Uniate clergy - I mean that that should be Russian,- likes "analogies" very much. The Popes have established "Holy days" and "traditions" and the Ugro-Russian Catholic ksendz Mikita was put to compose himself ad usum Delphini!... Another ksendz - Mellesh made up a Gregorian calender with Eastern Saints; the third one Pheslorii made up an alphabet shoving there in Latin letters the Russian primars per analogiam; in Galicia there was a "patriot" who composed a prayerbook written using Polish grammar. The Pope permits the Latin ksendzes to serve two Masses a day at the missions - and what happens - the Ugro-Russian Uniate ksendz per analogiam starts to serve three.- Instead of going with a missionary box around, he per analogiam carries nonsense around and sells water from Lourdes; etc. In other words, if the Galician "patriots" according to the resolutions made by the council of Lvov will become Latin-Papists of the 13th - Grade, then those will try per analogiam to be Catholics not lover than the 15th Grade!... As "Svoboda" keeps deep silence about the orders given about the American Uniates by the Propaganda and about resolutions of the Council

---

[67] Remark: That is a very funny thing - to serve a panikhida (requiem) for a schismatic in a Uniate church; to perform this service with the same "intention" as for a Pope's faithful Uniate? What would that tell to the Ksendz-Cardinal? And the American Uniates do not believe that they are not consistent! Taras Shevchenko was not that, and his dreams were different than those our "patriotes ukrainomen" attribute to him. His confession was Orthodoxy - and his Little-Russian language was not that kind of - "mixtum compositum", like the one that is used "for publishing "Svoboda" in Mount Carmel. Therefore what kind of relationship is there between "patriotes" of the frankist "race" and Shevchenko? And why do the Uniales have to go to the Orthodox Church when a memorial service is made there for the righteous soul of the unforgettable Fr. Ioann Naumovich? Why do those "palrioles" not hold a panikhida service there for him? Especially since Fr. Archpriest Ioann has many more accomplishments for the Galician-Russian people than Shevchenko has, especially,- if we will talk about that "independent nation", to which only the fantasy of ukrainomen gave such a title.

of Lvov approved by the Pope, so also does " our dear organ - Vieslnik" per analogiam that also does not know anything either: "Svoboda" has a "people's movement" and "enlightenment",- "our dear Organ" has its "common interests", "our dear Union" and its own "sights and prayers"... Among themselves "Svoboda" and "Viestnik" are always arguing, - but they suffer the same sickness: they falsely fight for the Russian people... [68]

FEAR HAS BIG EYES!

As the proverb says "there is only one step from greatness to ridiculousness". The truthfulness of this proverb was proven some days ago by the Hungarian government. Four or five people, Russians, former Uniates who reunited here in America to the Orthodox Church, went back to the Fatherland, to the village of Becherov, Saros district, in Hungary. [69]

They had not even had time to rest from their trip when the Hungarian gendarmes came, and searched their houses with the intention of finding the "proclamations of the All-Russian Czar", which were directed to all Hungarian and Galician Russians instructing them to wait for just a little while, suffering under the Hungarian - yoke and oppression, since soon the All-Russian, or, better said in the terminology of the Jewish-Hungarian press, "Moscow's Czar" will send his regiments, to take the mountainous part of Ugria and Galicia from Austria. Then there will be harmony and prosperity for the Rusins!...

The inquisition began... With the complete efficiency and bureaucracy of Hungarian-Jewish justice, the suspect returnees were put into prison and everything printed in the Russian language was confiscated, not only from them but from every one who had visited America.

It is well known that in Ugria almost all the press is in the hands of baptized and un-baptized Jews,- and that press hit the alarm! On a daily basis in the Hungarian newspapers in Europe and here in America, articles appeared with headlines in bold type and large letters: "Panslavic movements in the mountainous part of Ugria and in the Saros district". Much nonsense was written in those articles! Fear, which always has big eyes, has seen here completely unthinkable big things. There was no longer talk about "proclamations", but about Russian cannons and Cossacks... Maybe the people of Becherov carried them in their pockets from America?! In other words an uproar began, as if Austria was entering the next day a war against Russia!...

However, those who know the conditions in Ugria and the fanatical hate against everything connected with the Russian name, against that which is written in Russian letters, spoken

---

[68] Permit me to ask "Svoboda" and "Viestnik" - would it not be better, at least, for a while, to leave alone all those "people's movements" and "common interests" in view of the fact that Rome and its Jesuit politics against all Union agreements, bulls and breves conducts a new attack against the Faith, Church and Rite of the Russian people; and with united force to stand up for their defense and after getting convinced by everyday examples in the insidiousness and treachery of Rome and the Jesuits, to come finally to the conscience at least to tell frankly here to the Russian people, that their salvation is not in Rome, not in the Pope's bosom, but in the Orthodox Eastern Church!... Is it possible that these newspapers will continue to chatter about "peasant movements" and about "our common interests" until there will not be even one Russian Uniate left here, and "Svoboda" by "Viestnik" and "Viestnik" by "Svoboda" will be read?... Remember... Proximus ardet Ucalegon! - in almost all your parishes, even in God's churches, there are disagreements fights: the enemies of the Russian-Faith and Russian nationality are using this circumstance! You yourselves are helping them... Do not forget, that "Roma locuta et comedia finita" The 12th hour is approaching; save what can be still be saved!...

[69] "Copies of some of the original documents describing the sad events in the Carpathian village of Becherov were obtained by AARDM from some of the parishioners of St. Mary's Cathedral in Minneapolis.

or printed, will not be surprised by all those angry tricks by the Judas-Hungarians. Even the simple salutation used by the Rusins to each other, "Slava Jisusu Christu" (Glory to Jesus Christ) outraged these people and now, - it is hard to believe, - it is forbidden to use this greeting! Here is one more example: the words from the Lord's prayer "Thy kingdom come"... raised the absurd suspicion, that these prayers are not about the Lord's Kingdom but for the Russian Kingdom! To speak Russian publicly became - Muscovite; to write, let's say, a birth-certificate or the minutes of a clergy meeting in Russian became treason against the state!...

Under such circumstances it is understandable, that the Hungarian administration did not stand on ceremony with the people of Becherov. But as much as they tried to find something, they could not find anything except harmless books and some Russian newspapers; they found not even a trace of "proclamations"! "A mountain bore a mouse" says the well-known proverb. The uproar slowly quieted down, and the talk about Panslavism also and the entire excitement became some kind of a childishly-funny raving by the Jewish press. Even some of the Jewish newspapers (not speaking about the Slavic) now found it comical that great chauvinism and stupidity made all these accusations possible.

And really:

1) Instead of proclamations it was found that the people of Becherov had Holy Scripture, prayerbooks, Akathists, pamphlets of religious-moral content, and even more, some of the latter items - were printed by the Kachkovski Society, therefore they were printed in Austria itself - not in Russia.

2) The "respected Pan " Michail Artim [70] in Becherov created the entire uproar which fooled the Hungarian government... He is a man of limited mind, not smart, but with a limitless vanity, who for a long time wished to be "somebody", to glorify himself in some way; but due to his limitations he could not achieve that. It came to his attention that the people in Becherov had collected here in America a small amount of money to build an Orthodox church in Becherov. [71] In every way he wished to stop this possibility, thinking to use those collected funds for gold plating the domes of his Uniate church. But it was in vain! He did not get the money and having revenge on his mind for their refusal to give

[70] *The rather anti-Jewish tone of this article by St. Alexis is due to the rather vehement- complaints and allegations of his former parishioners about the very unpleasant situation which arose when some of them returned to their homeland. The difficult conditions in the district of Saros had forced its citizens to move elsewhere to secure their livelihood or to morgage their properties with the local moneylender who happened to be a Jew. It is impossible, due to a shortage of documentation and reports of witnesses to recreate what really happened, but it appears that Fr. Artim was trying to maintain cordial relations both with his morgaged parishioners and with their mortgagor. As a result both Fr. Artim and the moneylender became very unpopular among the people.

[71] *Carpatians in the United States who had emigrated to Pennsylvania, Minnesota and Wisconsin began a collection of funds for an Orthodox chapel for Becherov where several Orthodox people had formed a commitee which petitioned the "Russkoe Pravoslavnoe Obchestvo Vsaimopomoschi" for financial assistance. Relatives and friends in America sent $600.00 for the chapel. Two brothers, Vasyl and Andrey Zbihly, arrived in Becherov with the money. They commited a grave mistake by their openness, shoving the local Uniale priest Artim their collection list and also the newspaper printed in America with the petition for help with the building fund for the chapel in Becherov. Fr. Artim did not like the possibility of competition in his parish and sent a message to the local gendarmerie about "Moscovites" who had come to Becherov to incite the people to revolt. In addition he also wrote a report to the Hungarian newspaper "Posti Hirlap" about events as he imagined them. The gendarmes confiscated from Vasyl and Andrey Zbihley their collection book and also their letters. They were accused of treason against the Hungarian State and other people from Becherov got involved - Vasyl Tutko, Ioann Banicky and others. The court in Presov decided that all these people did not commit any crime and released them from jail. But Fr. Artim was not happy with that outcome and continued his persecution of people who did not attend the Uniate church in the village. The two brothers left the country and went to Argentina, South America, where they began another colony with ties to the village of Becherov - known as Tres Copones - Kolonia (Colonia Azara) Teritorio Misiones. After some time with several more people from Becherov, they began to build a chapel there naming it the Holy Virgin Protectorate - the same name as the churches in Minneapolis, Minnesota in the United States and in Becherov, Carpathia

48

him the money, he invented a stupid fable about state treason and the proclamations of theRussian Czar, knowing well, that there was nothing else that would as easily excite the Hungarians as their fear of the Russians. [72]

3) The Hungarian governmental newspapers purposely blew up this rumor about the "Panslavic movement", having in mind their goal: to hurt the so-called "People' Party" (the opposition party in the Hungarian Parliament) before the coming elections; however,- isn't it strange- that the "Peoples" party doesn't have anything in common with the Russians or the Slavic nationality: that it is simply a party of Roman-Catholics and its representatives hate the Slavs as much as the other Hungarians do.

4) It did not matter that the manoeuvres of several stupid people was so absurd; never-less, the Hungarian minister Sayl has prohibited the bringing of the American-Russian news-paper "Svet" to Ugria; and he decided to send to America a Hungarian Police Chief with the title of "Hungarian-Greek-Catholic Biscup or Vicar" to stop the Orthodox movement among the Russian immigrants from Ugria and Galicia!

His plan was as follows: the Ugro-Rusins, up until now were in darkness and under a yoke; they could not achieve a national consciousness by themselves but would lose completely their heritage and become Hungarians. Helping the Hungarian politicians in this good deed would be the Uniate biskup and ksendzes, who as ad normam Michail Artim in Becherov were always ready to sell out their people and who were feeding them to the Jewish-Hungarian Moloch...

But at the same time the Ugro-Rusins who reunited with the Holy Orthodox Church learned in a short time, what "Unia" was and what kind of great benefits it brought them, - they came to the conclusion, that for them the name "Uniate" is shameful and disgraceful; that Unia kills not only their conscience but also their nationality - and praise the Lord for this; they woke up from a deadly sleep, and now even in their own land they plan to have an Orthodox church! The same Orthodoxy is confessed also by the Great-Russian people; and that is what is consid-ered by the Hungarians and Austrians as dangerous! That is the reason that they persecute everyone who reunited in America with the Orthodox Church!

The Hungarian-Austrian government brags to the entire world about their "liberalism", having passed against the will of the population laws for civil marriages and nonconfessionalism, better to call it unbelief; but at the same time they persecute people who have reunited with the Orthodox Church - that is, returned to the Church of their Great-grandfathers, from which they were torn away by force and fraud. That behavior contradicts the imagined liberalism and exhibits itself for ridicule,- does that stop them? How can a logical and just behavior be expected at all from a Hungarian or a Polack when a Jew sits on his neck? They are only consistent in one matter - in the continuation of their mean deed, which began 300 years ago. By the use of mean methods the ill-starred Unia was forced upon the Ugro and Galician Russian people,- now it can only be preserved by force and the use of jails! Then there were several biskup and priests who were with-out shame, who sold out their people,- and now as we see it is still being done. They do those deeds to receive material benefits and glory from the enemies of their people! The lineage of Terletzkys and Polzeys and other traitors did not die, but lives until our days under other names!... Their deeds and exploits also live.

---

[72] * Fr. Artim saw the Rusins who returned from the United States as a threat; that his Uniate church would receive less income, and that the villagers would no longer work as much on his land and for his household. Now there were some villagers who could read and write and therefore did not need his assistance anymore. The "Moscovites" as he called the people who were returning from Minneapolis were revolutionaries, according to him, who rejected his authority in the village. One of them even mentioned that one of them would, after studying in Minnea-polis, become an Orthodox priest.

THE ARCHPRIEST JOHN NAUMOVICH
AS VIEWED BY THE UNIATE VIESTNIK

Whoever is not convinced by this time, that the "Viestnik of our dear Union", intentionally fogs and mixes up the American-Russian people, has only to read its recent article,- one of the most foolish ones that has ever appeared on the pages of that newspaper rag. That article's title is - "Knowledge for us, the American-Rusins". There are many cock and bull stories on the conscience of the editors and also malicious lies, but the above mentioned article is probably the most shameless.

"Alexis Toth",- said that "Knowledge", - "is a real impostor(?) and his company(?), have because of great poverty and for profiteering renounced their faith(?) to find means for their gentry-like life. They are using our people, calling them to join, and for this reason they blacken and ridicule everything that our people do..."

What kind of rubbish and nonsense is all this? Did I ever hide my program, which I have used as the basis of my Orthodox missionary activity? Did I not openly teach and am teaching now, that Unia is a spiritual yoke for the Russians from Hungary and Galicia? Therefore if we want to stay Russian not only in words but in deeds we have to free ourselves from Rome, which takes away from us our faith, our nationality, our church, our cross and our monasteries. I also said that the people should not listen to parasites, ex-village notaries, who were only half-educated, who can neither read nor write Russian, but who want to be enlighteners and to live in all kinds of Unions as gently, with the money paid by the callused hands of poor working Rusins. This is my conviction and this is what I fight for... Did I establish the Holy Orthodox Church and Faith?... And if now by the Grace of God, our people have found the true Knowledge and reunite with the Holy Orthodox Church, then your shameless, lying reproach is not my denunciation; it is turned into your eternal dishonor and curse!...

What kind of material advantages do I receive from my - business? - I remain, as long as I live, the same as I am today... My "interests are advantageous for everyone" - not some kind of nonsense for a bankbook, like water from Lourdes and other things, - don't forget that!... What I have achieved until now was with God's help, - and it is good. Where the Russians heard my weak call and returned to their Mother - Orthodox Church, - there are no scandals among them and people feel themselves true Russians. The first proof of that is your own - wild, angry attack and slander, that I despise and loath. But I am going at the same time my own way, the road of truth and goodness...

Your accuse me of "blackening and ridiculing everything that the people do"... Don't you call yourself "these people"? If you are the "people" then what are you "doing" that has to be praised and not censured.? What comes from you are acts of meanness, badness, dishonesty!... Who is it that makes our poor people blind, but you yourself?... If they are spiritually blind until now, is that their fault? Is it not the fault of such people as you, who never told them a word of truth?... Like a thief the inglorious Unia came into their churches; no one asked the people if they agreed to renounce their great great grandfather's faith. Several centuries ago, to obtain benefits and honors, several traitors committed an outrageous insult to that which was most holy in the lives of people when they started Unia... You use now the same methods; your actions are driven by a desire for the same material benefits and they push you to the same crimes against the truth and against the people... And therefore you use the same type of measurement for the infamous beginning of your goals, and the more foolish the people are, the better it is for you... Do not hide yourself behind the "people"!

Am I not telling the truth? Is it not your "Knowledge" that, supposedly the Hungarian and Galician-Russians - are something different than the "Moscovites", the people of Great Russia? - that supposedly the Orthodox Faith is worse than the pagan, that supposedly it is "schismatic"? - that supposedly the Orthodox Church acknowledges neither the Holy Trinity, nor the Theotokos? - that supposedly "rimskaja i greckaja vera are vsicho jedno" (the same), and so on, and so on?... And finally in addition to all of that you send "memorandums" to all ends of the earth but at the same time establish Greek Catholic Calvinism in Philadelphia!... Are my words not true?...

I fought with my accusations against such falsehood but you, instead, to prove to me that I am wrong, that I am casting aspersions,- repeat the words of I. Dubina in the newspaper "Svet", "and are becoming personal and are attacking personality"!... I can always show a place and time, and a name, and object, when, and where, and how and who of you has committed meanness, - and what about you?... When I write something, I sign it, I show my face,- but what about you? Without honor you hide behind someone else's name. But you can't hide your long ears!...

Drawing a parallel between me and the great well - known man, to whom according my realization, I am not worthy to untie the laces of his shoes, Rev. Fr. Archpriest I. Naumovich,- you tell about him and about Michael Kachkovski, that "even though in spirit and body they were Russian, they were teaching Greek-Catholic-Uniate Russian people; but they never said even a word never mentioned, that the people should renounce their faith and accept Orthodoxy"...

What kind of shameless lie is that! Has Judas' hate killed the last drop of your conscience? Is it possible that you wish even to distort such facts as the entire world knows? Then why did Fr. John Naumovich fight, if not for the faith and nationality? Did not people in Hnilichi and Skolat return to Holy Orthodoxy at his call? Was that not the reason that he and those people suffered persecution and imprisonment in jails? Was it not for that, that he was anathematized by the rancorous Cardinal Sembratowicz, and then by the Pope? Was that not the reason that the Austro-Polish governments accused and hanged - hochverath (high treason) on his neck and the necks of the people of Hnilichki and Skolat?... - Was it not for that reason that they r e n o u n c e d U n i a? And for what reason,- then, did Fr. John Naumovich go to Russia? Was it to be a Uniate?... No; being convinced, that only the Orthodox faith can save the Galician-Russian people, he went to Russia, where he as an Archpriest pursued his goal for the goodness of the Galician-Russian people, and in that rank he gave his pious soul to the Lord. His grave is at the Askoldov cemetery, in Kiev. Why have you so impudently hushed and twisted this all up?... That is what you are always doing to everything. You write about Fr. Naumovich for the Russian people and hide the most important moment in his life; you are not ashamed to lie, that supposedly he never "said even a word nor mentioned to the people to accept Orthodoxy!... [73]

That is how enlighteners of the Galician-Russian lands were paid! The poor and tortured people deep in their hearts preserve Fr. Naumovich and Kachkovski, while their present "leaders", who plan to receive a "patent" for their patriotism, and who teach their "enlightenment on the basis of Franko-Dragomanov ideas" twist the memories of these people.

I will say this once more: if there were no Holy Orthodox Mother - Russia, religious and a true preserver of the Faith and Rite,- then there would be no a place for Rev. Fr. Naumovich to lay his head; if there would not be the most pious sovereign of Russia,- then his family would also not have their daily bread!... Unia with its lecherous patriots of the new era and with its "gentrified brothers" have torn people apart in the Old Country; and here in America, the knights of the same Unia continue the same loathsome work... Now after all that you decorate the pages of your vulgar and untruthful newspaper with pictures of these enlighteners of the Galician Rus'?... Yes, indeed Fr. Naumovich suffered many deep mortifications during his life; now after his death the Uniate false-patriots have not ceased insulting him with their "praises"!...

Let's return to the parallel, which I would not dare under any circumstances make on my own initiative,- between that glorious and eternal enlightener, Fr. Naumovich, and me; since you did that, than I should be allowed to say several words per analogiam...

I was a Uniate when I came to America; as a former professor of Church law, I knew, that here in America as a Uniate priest I had to obey the Roman Catholic biscup of the particular diocese in which I happened to serve; the conditions of Unia demand this, as well as various Papal bulls, brevets and decretalias, since there was and there is not until now a Uniate biscup here. Moreover, in my credentials - litterae accreditive - the following istruction was clearly written: "Dilectio tua debet semet personalites coram Praesule istius Dioceseos presentare, in cuius teritorio habetur locus destinationis suae". The place of my appointment was Minneapolis,

---

[73] Then finally why don't you say also to the people that Michael Kachkovski is resting in eternal sleep in the great Russian land, in the city of Kronstadt?

Minn., in the diocese of Archbiskup Ireland.[74] As an obedient Uniate, I complied with the orders of my bishop, who at that time was John Valiy, and appeared before Ireland on December 19, 1889, kissed, as I should have, his hand according to custom (failing, however, to kneel before him, which as I learned later was my chief mistake) and presented to him my credentials. I remember well, that no sooner did he read that I was a "Greek-Catholic", than his hands began to shake! It took him almost 15 minutes, to read to the end, after which he asked me abruptly (the conversation was in the Latin language):

-"Do you have a wife?"
-"No!"
-"But you had one?"
-"Yes, I am a widower..."

Hearing this, he threw the paper on the table and loudly shouted:

-"I have already written to Rome protesting against this kind of priest being sent to me..."
-"What kind of priest do you mean?"
-"Your kind."
-"But I am a Catholic priest of the Greek Rite, I am a Uniate, and I was ordained by a lawful Catholic bishop."
- "I do not consider that either you nor that bishop are Catholic; besides, I do not need any Greek Catholic priests here; a Polish priest in Minneapolis is more than enough. He can also be the priest for the Greeks"...
-"But he belongs to the Latin Rite; besides, our people will not understand him and so they will hardly go to him; that was the reason that they built a church of their own"...
-"I did not give them permission to do that, and I do not grant you jurisdiction to serve here"... I was deeply hurt by this kind of fanaticism of this representative of Papal Rome and sharply replied to him:
-"In that case I neither ask from you a jurisdiction, nor your permission; I know the rights of my Church, I know the basis on which Unia was established, and I will act according to them..." The Archbiskup lost his temper. I lost mine just as much. One word led to another; the thing so far that it is not worthwhile to reconstruct our entire conversation further. Two days later, Jacob Pacholsky, who was the Polish ksendz came to me, and as if he was terrorstricken, said:
-"For God's sake, Your Reverence, what have you done? A priest from the Archbishop wrote me, that I must not have any communication with you, the Archbishop does not accept you as a lawfully ordained priest, and I am now under strict orders from him to announce this at the altar, - to forbid your people to ask you for church services and to receive from you sacraments"...
-"This is your concern, - do what you wish to do, but I will not step even a step back, and it does not make any difference to me, what the Archbiskup or you will do..." [75]

---

[74] *A copy of the original appointment is located in Supplement, see Documents 1 1, 2 and 3

[75] I was meeting Fr. Jacob Pacholsky often. He had already suggested to me to contact "the Pan-Slavic Catholics", who were in great number in Minnesota and who speak all the time about an independent Slavic state. From him I obtained an address of a church in Hopkins, Minnesota. I contacted the priest and the curators of the church and found out that they were Czechs and in Minnesota they were living around New Prague, Heidelberg, Silver Lake, Litonysl, Winona, and other places, all parishes established between the end of the 50's through the 90's of this century. They did not have the same difficulties as did I, since they were of Latin Rite; they were also helped in establishing their churches by other Catholics, but their difficulty was the same in that the bishop here was sending to their parishes German and Polish priests, who were against their own national culture. I spoke about all that with Fr. Jacob and he told me all about the difficulties that the Polish parishes have with the Irish bishops and told me to have patience. He also told me that the local Catholic seminary in St. Paul headed by Bishop Ireland who recently started it with the help of Gorman, Mc Sweeny, Keane and Byrne, has recruited only West Europeans to teach there. That immediately struck me like a lightning bolt, that during my meeting with the Bishop, when I told him that I knew my rights as a Catholic, since I was a professor at the theological seminary in Hungary, the Bishop said then that in those seminaries they did not teach what the Catholic religion is.

The demands of the Archbiskup were made public,- he sent his complaints to Rome, and my parishioners were getting scared, that the Archbiskup will chase their priest etc. In the meantime I received letters from several of my fellow-priests, Uniates, who all wrote me that many of them, were treated just as I had been by Latin biskup and ksendzes. I informed the Uniate biscup in Priashev, asking his instructions, but he never answered me! Naturally not! Would a Uniate bishop dare to contradict a Latin Rite archbiskup?!... I wrote a second and third time, still without obtaining any reply! At last I received from Canon Joseph Dzubay the following instruction: "...for God's sake, be patient; and if the Archbiskup doubts that you are a faithful Catholic, let him know that you are willing to take your oath on it!"...

After a while I received another letter from him, proposing that I write a detailed account of the way the Archbiskup received me and advised me to write the report very carefully, as the report would be sent to Rome... This I did; but later on, the same Dzubay informed me that the truth was too harshly described in my report to be sent to Rome. However, some measures were taken and Rome was told that the Latin Rite bishops should respect Holy Unia...

In the meantime, the convention at Wilkes-Barre took place on October 15-27, 1890. As result of the protocols of this convention, the remonstrances of two bishops, and my own complaints, Rome that is, the Propaganda Fide, sent an answer: all of us should be recalled from America!

What should be done? I called my parishioners together and explained to them the sad position we were in, explaining that under these conditions it certainly was best that I leave them.

-"No," - said some of them, - "let's go to the Russian bishop, why should we always submit ourselves to foreigners!"...

-"All right," I said,- "but where does the Russian bishop live? And what is his name?"

Some people said that he lives in Alaska, in Sitka,- the others said in San Francisco... I myself knew absolutely nothing, except that a Russian Consul lived in San Francisco! Therefore, using the name of the reader Michael Potochnak, I sent the following inquiry to the Russian consulate: "Is it true that a Russian Orthodox Bishop lives in San Francisco? If so, what is his name and where does he live?"- In 10 days a letter arrived addressed to Michael Potochnak, informing him that the name of the Prelate is His Grace Bishop Vladimir, and that he lives at 1715 Powell Street North, San Francisco. This was on 6/18 December of 1890. After that, we decided to send a collector [76] into the far West, that he might personally verify this information and also request a contribution from the Bishop for the installation of an iconostasis, since at that time we in the Minneapolis church did not have one. It was more important however to find out if he really was an Orthodox bishop, and not some kind of Old Believer. [77] Ivan (John) Mlinar was selected as the collector and he went to San Francisco. He arrived safely in San Francisco and went to the cathedral. There he started to talk with the now deceased cathedral abbot George Chudnovsky!... To the abbot's question about his religion, Mlinar answered that he was taught in school that he is of the "Orthodox Greek-Catholic Russian Faith". As it turned out the abbot was a Little-Russian and could talk with him without difficulty.- Mlinar was admitted to the bishop, who examined his collection book, and presented him with 10 dollars. There was no chance for the collector to talk with his Grace, until there was a chance for that. Mlinar, as a member of the brotherhood, wished to have confession before the Nativity of Christ holiday and the now deceased Fr. Abbot received his confession, but the next day, when he came for the Holy Sacrament of Communion, Protodeacon Fr. John Sobolev (now he is a priest and pastor in Alaska), who heard something about Mlinar from Fr. Abbot, indicated to his Grace the Bishop, that in his opinion Mlinar might be a Uniate?... Then in church in front of everyone, the Bishop asked Mlinar, who he is? Mlinar answered again as above. But from the questions that followed, it was found out that he is indeed a Uniate. Then the Bishop gave him instruction in

---

[76] * It is customary in Orthodox parishes to send a person to collect funds from other Orthodox anywhere whenever the church needs a large amount of money for a particular purpose such as building a monastery, a school, etc. These people are called collectors.

[77] Such an assumption was based on some reports in articles in American newspapers that there were some kind of settlements of Russian Cossacks along the Pacific coast. That was also the reason for me to send the request not in my priestly name, but in the name of a layman.

a fatherly way and said that even though he is a Russian, but his faith is Catholic and he belongs to the Uniate sect and that his Archpastor is - the Roman-Catholic biscup, then he has to get confession and communion from him. That time Mlinar was not permitted to receive communion! Mlinar immediately went to the local Catholic archbiskup, but as soon as his secretary - a ksendz, saw in his collection book, that he is a "Greek-Catholic" he sent him back to "his own Russian bishop on Powel Street!"

The letter that Mlinar sent me on that occasion from San Francisco is very interesting; because of some language that he used I will not include it completely; but there will be enough, two or three sentences, to judge the spiritual condition of the poor collector: "So what kind of unknown faith are we? We were taught and you teach us, that we are Orthodox people, and here the Orthodox bishop did not permit me to receive communion,- sent me to the Catholic biscup, and the Catholic biscup did not want to talk to me and chased me to the Russian bishop... Therefore, what kind of faith is this? I am told that I am a Uniate; what Uniate? I did not ever hear that before... I have always considered myself an Orthodox Christian?..."

He again went back to his Grace Vladimir and then in detail told about his misfortune and about our condition. Then his Grace Vladimir wrote me the following letter:

1-st day of January 1891
San Francisco, California

To the priest and Church Warden Polochny and all parishioners [78]
of the Russian church in the city of Minneapolis.
From Vladimir, Bishop of the Aleutian and Alaskan diocese:
Communication

Grace and peace be with you from our Lord Jesus Christ dear countrymen!

Having received your request about assistance for your church with icons and either things, I have difficulty in responding to you positively, since you have not notified me; - who are you: Orthodox, or Uniates of the Pope - falsely-infallible? Who is your bishop?
If you are Orthodox, do you wish to be included in the Alaskan Diocese?
Write to me about this immediately.

The Lord's blessing be with you!
Vladimir Bishop of the Aleuts and Alaska.

* * * * *

Remark: But a week before receiving this letter, I received the following letter from Fr. Abbot Chudnovsky. As it happened: Fr. Abbot believed Mlinar; that he and the people who sent him - are Orthodox, and the misunderstanding came later.

The Russian Ecclesiastical Consistory of Alaska[79]
12/24 day Dec. 1890
San Francisco, California

Peace and the Lord's Blessing be with us Most Reverend colleague and brother in Christ, Father Alexis Yurievich Toth!
Today Mister Ivan Mlinar, parishioner of your Holy Virgin Protection Church came to me and showed his collection book. He told me about your needs.

---

[78] A copy of the original is located in Supplement, see document 1 4
[79] A copy of the original is located in supplement, see document 1 5.

54

It made me happy to hear, that besides our churches in San Francisco and in Northern Alaska, by the Grace of the Lord, there is also another Orthodox church in the city of Minneapolis, where you have been the pastor for more than a year, but at the same time I am sorrowful that until now you do not know us, nor we, you: and the church can not exist without a bishop, as the bishop cannot without the Synod or the Patriarch. And therefore I write to you as a brother to a brother, let's get acquainted; write in detail about yourself; but it would be even better, if you could by means of your Orthodox Society, personally come to visit our Bishop Vladimir and talk to him about all matters interesting to you.

> The God of Peace and Love be with us forever!
> The Cathedral Church of St. Basil
> Abbot George Chudnovsky

After the return of Mlinar to Minneapolis, and following the suggestion of Fr. Abbot, in the beginning of February I myself went to San Francisco accompanied by the church warden Paul Podany, and with the agreement of my wordy flock. The result of my travel there was that the Most Reverend Bishop Vladimir came to us and on March 25, 1891 reunited all of us into the bosom of our great great grandfather's Orthodox Church; but as was said before, only in October of 1892 were we accepted into the membership of the Aleutian and Alaska diocese, according to a resolution of the Holy Ruling All-Russian Synod! The time from March 25, 1891 until October of 1892 was full of sorrow conscience I can say that rarely in my life have I had to suffer so many grievances as at that time!...[80]

I had not considered writing about all those events, at least not now, but I am forced to do so by the Uniate clergy, with a small exception! - There is a hopeless condition in their position, which is becoming sectarian, and at the same time they make the air dirty, using all kinds of slander and unsubstantiated statements; making trouble and gossiping; accusing me of joining Holy Orthodoxy for "business", for my own material advantages! The organ of the "dear Union" and the Ukrainophils' "Svoboda" shout about that to the entire world... Therefore, let everyone know, how and why the idea came to my mind and how reuniting with our native Church became a reality!...

You, - the false brothers, do think and assume, that it is very easy, as it is for a bird, to fly from one place to another, or to serve, whispering 2-3 liturgies a day, to change your Church?... No! - Hard minutes of my life! I had to live through them; I know then against what and whom I would have to wrestle and deal! But the Lord gave me the power to struggle first with myself and win; to cease to be a disdained slave of the Pope. Unia with all its meanness and poison has not killed in me the feelings of sensitivity and reasoning so much that I would with Muslim fatalism suffer all that, which the Uniates until now have suffered from their "protectors"!...

Glory be to our Lord for His great mercy!

There is a question - do not the local advocates of this "Unia" right here know about this oppression? As it seems, they do not leave Unia, no! but it is because of their own direct advantages that they even continue to support it. Otherwise all these idiocies would already be given to a "second hand" store! And therefore you yourself have to judge - who is doing "business", me or your own "cobrothers"?!...

In conclusion I will also remark:

1) The contemporaries of these events are still alive - who doubts the truth of my words should ask them; - yes, besides that all the original papers, documents are until now in my possession and I will show them to any one...

2) The "Viestnik of our dear Union" is twaddling: "we are considered the best (?) Rusins-Russians here; better than the impostor Alexis Toth and his company (who is that?), since we are Russians (?) from birth (? oh! oh!). We are Russians (?!) in conviction (?!) (nonsense, slops, etc?), and not for "business"... To all that I will only tell: nobody ever saw that I made "business" serving two liturgies or making non-sense, including exhibiting icons of St. Nicholas, one with

---

[80] * Fr. A. Toth published with this article following in the supplement documents No. 6-9.

a beard and another one without, with "miraculous water from Lourdes" etc; - I did not bless Paskha bread (kulichi) in stoves, or even when they were still in the form of dough, I am not an editor of any publication which would speak against my personal beliefs and would not work there for my support; I have never been a "secretary" of a Union nor an "overseer of a newspaper". I do not ride a bicycle for collections. Did any one see me doing that? And have you seen your Uniate ksendzes doing these nonsenses?

3) I agree with the words of the weak-minded editor of the Union newspaper: "But we in America have a problem since we have many people here 'who close peoples' eyes, so that they would not see the light of the truth, and the people would live with their eyes lightly closed', and continue to serve the interests of those people and not know their own people, who wish them well. They throw stones at those who would wish to cover them with goodness and to lead them to the right road of their own!"...

I will explain only: "the peoples' eyes are tightly closed" indeed by rags and shawls like the Uniate "Viestnik" and "Svoboda"; and as "business" no one else but those of poor spirit and head work for the daily bread and to the advantage of their patrons of nonsense, and the advocate of "our own interest", and the inventor of the "Greek-Catholic language", who is fed with the bread of "our dear Union" by the money of its members.

FROM THE HISTORY OF THE CHURCH AND PARISH IN MINNEAPOLIS.

The church and parish in Minneapolis was established by the immigrants from Austro-Hungary,- Russians by nationality, Uniate by faith. In 1882, the first to come here were, Yuri Homzik and Theodore Sivanich,- both from Strebnik, Sharishsky County. [81] Year after year there have come after them other people from there. [82]

The Uniates who arrived in Minneapolis in their spiritual and church necessities were going either to the German Papal ksendz [83] who was by nationality a Croat or they went to the Polish ksendz, who understood more their Little-Russian language. Even the above named Theodore Sivanich did much to build the Polish kostel. The Polish ksendz was trying in any way to take control of the Uniates: he was speaking about them as about Polacks... and the unknowing,

---

[81] * The founder of the Uniate Russian Community in Minneapolis was George Homzik, who arrived in 1877 at the age of 27. He married a newly arrived immigrant Paula and by 1905 they had 10 children. Theodore Sivanich came to Minneapolis in 1880 at age 25. Before this there were already some other Russians here but they had not formed a community.
In 1849, Minnesota had become a territory and in 1850 the 7 th census of the United States showed that there were 6,038 white and 39 black people there. (Indians were not counted.) Among the white population in Minnesota, 2 people were listed as from the Russian Empire. One was Mark Issac, a salesman, 27 years old. It is not known from what part of Russia he came. His name suggests that he was probably Jewish. The other immigrant was Martin Fitcourt, 60 years old, a worker from Poland. (Minnesota Territorial Census, 1850, edited by Patricia C. Harpole, Minnesota Historical Society, St. Paul, 1972, pp. 6 and 44.) According to the census of 1860, there were already 127 people from Poland and 59 from Russia in the territory. Those numbers are not exact because some people did not reveal their nationality and not all who came from the Russian Empire were Russian but were of different ethnic groups (Finns, Jews, Byelorussians, etc.) Also some Russians came to the United States by passing through the Austro-Hungarian Empire and because of that it was shown in their papers that they were Austrian, Hungarian, Bohemian, Slovac, Polish, etc. in origin.

[82] * They came from the villages of Beherov, Komlos, and Strebnik in the Carpatian Mountains of Austria and Hungary, from the part which was later known as Czechoslovakia, and were known as Carpatho-Russians or Ugro-Russians.

[83] The kostel where he served was located on the corner of 2nd Street and 7th Avenue N.E.

ignorant, non-educated people have been calling themselves not Russians,but either "Polanders", or Bohemians...! This has to be attributed to the circumstance, that in Hungary the government has demoralized and dispirited the Russian people so much, that they were ashamed to be Russians. Besides this there people were seeing disrespect toward the priests and the churches of the unfortunate Uniates, they instinctively were feeling, their bad position. And it could have happened, that the immigrants who arrived here and who were separated from the others in Pa., under the influence of the Polish ksendz - Jacob Poholsky would all have become in short time Latin Papists, but God's Providence sent to America a Uniate priest from Lvov Father Ivan Voliansky who settled down in Shenandoah, Pa., and from there he visited the Russian Uniates: he baptized them, confirmed them and most important he strengthened them in their faith and their nationality. And so in 1888 he arrived in Minneapolis.

The 80 Uniates who were living here, were requesting the German and the Polish ksendz to allow them in their kostel to make a service to the Lord, but the Archbiskup of St. Paul in whose territory Minneapolis was located, simply prohibited the performance of the service, explaining his prohibition, that making a service according to the Eastern rite would arouse a scandal among his faithful!... However a liturgy was celebrated in a private house owned by Paul Podany and George Homzik, there they had their confession and communion... The Archbiskup, by name John Ireland made rude attacks against Father Ivan Voliansky however this circumstance only helped the Russians; they united and thanks to the work of Theodore Sivanich, George Homzik, and Piotr Kuchechka, decided to build for themselves a church. Among themselves they collected donations and sent to Pennsylvania Piotr Podany as a fund raiser. The collected funds allowed them in 1888 to build a church, which was in 1889 blessed by the above mentioned Father Voliansky in honor of the Protection of the Holy Virgin,- this happened in the spring when the first service to the Lord was made there. In the summer came Father Alexander Dzubay who suggested to the people that they should call for themselves a priest. [84] It has been difficult but finally the people agreed and they called Father Ian Zapatotsky from the Priashev diocese who finally came to America, but stayed in Kingston, Pa. making the people in Minneapolis very sad. In place of Zapatotsky on the 27th of November, 1889 came I, the writer of this history, Alexis G. Toth, also a priest from the diocese of Priashev. I found the church built, however being empty: there was really nothing inside. I began to ask for charity from my people and people of other faiths to supply the church with the most important items. There were 14 families and several single people, all together 89 souls who were parishioners of the church. I prayed to God and God, especially the most Holy Virgin Mary, didn't abandon me, during a year, I collected so much that I could buy 5 vestments, a Gospel, a shroud of Christ, candleholders, gonfalons, icons, a chalice, and other things; everything together cost $ 840. In 1890 I bought for $1500 a house for the priest, and paid the $ 1800 debt, so that the parish house and the church were worth more than $ 7000 and today, when I am writing this, there are no other debts except $1980. There was much work, and unpleasantness, and I do not want to talk about it only God alone knows about it... Our people who came to America, oppressed in their home in Hungary, got here full liberty, which they understood poorly, and they explained to themselves that they, as free people, do not have any responsibilities even toward God!... And they started to look on their priest as only on their servant... They were not paying me: and so I had to leave and to suffer need, but always I have been calling God's name: and I didn't lose heart and didn't fall into despair. The most unpleasantness and struggle I had with the Papists, that started from the Archbiskup immediately after my arrival who gave an order to his Polish ksendz to read in the Polish kostel, that he doesn't consider me a Catholic, nor a priest, that all my activity is meaningless, and he was warning, and even simply prohibiting, the Russians to go to their church!...

But everything was in vain... Seeing my activity and that even also such people, who had become before almost complete Latin Papists were now returning to their people and that the number of my faithful was every day larger, the Archbiskup proclaimed my excommunication and demanded from the Roman Congregation de Propaganda Fide, that the Uniate bishop of Priashev Ian Valosh would recall me to the homeland,- especially for the reason,

---

[84] *Father Alexander Dzubay returned later to Orthodoxy and became a bishop under the monastic name Stephen.

that I have been exciting other Russian Uniate priests in America, calling on them to preserve the rights against the attacking biskups...

When I saw all of that, when I heard of that, then I made a decision to do such a thing, that had been already long in my heart to do something which my spirit was demanding!... To become Orthodox!... But how could I do that? I have had to be very careful... Unia, this unfortunate Unia which was the beginning of decline and of all badness, was already very rooted among our people. 250 years passed since that yoke was put on our necks!... I was from the bottom of my heart praying to the Lord that He would provide me help and strength to explain to my uneducated faithful. And God heard my prayer: I began to teach people and I sent a trusted one Ian Mlinar to the Orthodox Bishop Vladimir of the Aleutian Islands and Alaska who as I learned was at that time in San Francisco to find out; wouldn't he accept us under his authority?... After that on the 11th of February 1891, I took the long road myself (6 days by railroad). And finally the Bishop himself came to us on the day of the Triumph of Orthodoxy on the 25th of March and united us with Orthodoxy, altogether 361 souls. The people who were called and to whom everything was explained with loud voices denounced the wrong-teaching of the Papal church, and we returned there, from where our forefathers were separated by lie, by flattery, by force and by malice... Glory to the Lord for His grace to us! I knew, that the Papists will not let it pass in silence. And immediately there started to thunder condemnations in these kostels,- especially in the Polish... The Archbiskup again condemned by damnation. There was no such means which was not used against me: it was sad that I sold the Christian faith to the "Muscovites" for 30,000 Rubles, that I am a cheater, that I am a thief, who stole the orphans' money in Hungary and run to America... In other words the entire arsenal of Papal cunning and malice was used against me. The dressed-in-civil Jesuit ksendzes started to visit secretly my people and excite them. Some of the people began to have doubts and to my unhappiness the Holy Synod at that time recalled Bishop Vladimir to Russia; I stayed here without protection. The Uniate biskup of Priashev recalled me home, I disobeyed, being already at that time Orthodox. He blackened me giving a bad description about me, giving my name to the Great condemnation and sent all of that to the local Polish ksendz and archbiskup. The people were not paying me anything: I have had need in everything but I believed firmly that the Lord will not leave me without His mercy!...

In March in 1892 in my sad condition as in a clouded sky appeared a shining sun... The news arrived that to our Orthodox was appointed the Most Reverend Bishop Nicholas who had already come to America! God give me to see better days!...

ⲓⲥ ⲭⲥ

58

The sermon of Saint Alexis,

Pastor of the Orthodox Russian parish in the city of Minneapolis on August 16, 1892 after receiving the decree from the Holy Synod about acceptance into the Aleutian Diocese.

Orthodox Christians,

With these words I congratulate you now; since now with just basis and right I can give you that name! On Thursday, late evening, joyful news came to us, that our hope, our wish, that we waited to happen for a long 20 months, is realized, that our dear Mother, from which our ancestors and forefathers 244 years ago - that is in 1648, in Uzhorod were forcibly separated, again accepts us into her bosom; you know whom I talk about? - The Orthodox Church!... Christ's Church, the only Holy Ecumenical Apostolic Church, and by whom were we returned? By the Holy Ruling Synod, by the presentation of our Most Reverend Lord and Father - Bishop Nicholas, with the Sovereign's agreement , the most pious and most mighty Great Emperor - the Russian Monarch! - What kind of feeling must this happy new arouse in us? - A feeling of gratitude to God, and then to the Holy Synod, and to the important and great people named by me! You know well, that we had to suffer, how we were persecuted by those, who told, that we are one with them - the Uniates; they wished to take away from us everything that had been most important for us in the world. - The Church, Rite, our nationality... It seemed to them even much that, which they left us!... Even here, in the free American Land, where thanks to the glorious American People and their government, anyone can be in liberty, by one's own free will, to glorify God and confess, as he wishes. - Only it was not permitted to us! And therefore we called from the bottom of our souls to that Mother, whom we were forced to leave! And she heard the voice that called her!... And she embraced us again and accepted us as her children!... I taught you and not once told you, what Christ's Church teaches; my teaching has been confirmed by two Bishops, two true successors and inheritors of the Apostles... You have seen them, you have heard their word, you received blessings from them. Not long ago our Most Reverend Bishop and Father, here in our modest and poor church mercifully promised us that he would do his utmost and would not forget us - and the word became deed. What was said by our Bishop happened, and we are already Orthodox, we became his sons and by him we are sons of the Holy Mother Church!... we are now under the administration of that Holy Synod, that is administering millions of Orthodox people in Europe, Asia and America! And the most important is that getting under the administration of the Holy Synod, we are uniting spiritually with our own brothers - not only in faith, but by nationality - with the great, mighty, glorious, pious - Russian Nation! How much I told you already about sacred places in this great nation; these sacred places are now also ours, we will not be strangers there if we would come to pray to our Lord and to the Holy Ones who pleased God in Moscow, Kiev... we will be there at home, there are Russians there, there is Orthodoxy, there is uprightness, there is truth! Indeed, we are separated by distance, a sea is between that blessed country, where people there pray to truthful God, and where rules the most pious great Lord, the Russian Emperor, to whom we have to be grateful even though he is not ruling over us, since his protective hand spreads also over us; he mercifully permitted the Holy Synod to accept us into the Orthodox Church; the glorious American Land makes us free, to which we also have to be grateful from the bottom of our hearts, its government is our government that is in friendly relations with the great Russian people and to its Emperor crowned from above!...

Orthodox people! Remember, that even though the Russian Emperor is not our Sovereign, but he is Protector of all Orthodox people and he is Hope to all enslaved Russians and Slavs. Therefore we have always to pray for him, for his long happy administration, for his Royal House, for the Empress and his heir, - let's pray for the Holy Synod, who mercifully has accepted us, let's pray for the Most Reverend Bishop Vladimir, who showed us the road of the truth, and especially let's pray for our Most Reverend Bishop Nicholas, who has accomplished the good deed, by whose request we achieved our goal! Lord protect Him for us for many good years in safety and well being! And we will by good, peaceful and Christian lives, love of God and His Church prove, that we are not only in words, but also in hearts - truthful children of the Orthodox Church, - God and the Orthodox Church will not leave us, and the Lord's love will stay among us forever! Amen.

Saint Alexis' sermon, given at the church in Minneapolis.

IN THE NAME OF THE FATHER AND THE SON AND THE HOLY SPIRIT.

Orthodox people !

Today we celebrate the festivity of the Protection of the Mother of God. The Church is dedicated and blessed by this name, far from our Fatherland. But anyplace wher-ever we would be the Lord's Mother is with us! She hears our prayers to Her. She is also here in Minneapolis and she hears our prayers, She sees when you put candles before her icon requesting for yourself, your homeland and your friends Her assistance and protection.

Our forefathers from the eternal times have zealously celebrated this holiday. Our Rus' 900 years ago was a great and cultural state, confessing one religion. But then Rus' was divided into separate principalities and princes began not only to quarrel among themselves but even to fight each other. The Lord punished Rus' and the princes. From the East came the Mongolic horde - our forefathers were too weak because of their internal wars and besides that there was no unity among them. As a result they were conquered. For centuries Russians were taken to the slave markets, where they were sold.

Also at the Western borders of Rus' not everything was satisfactory. The Polish-Lithuanian state occupied all the lands of Rus' from our Carpathian mountains to the East including the capital of Kiev. In spite of all the solemn promises of the Polish Kings to equalize in rights our Church, its clergy and princes; the fanatical Polish gentry did not permit in Poland any equality to non-Poles. Our clergy was not permitted to take part in the Seims, our princes, their people and the Cossacks were excluded in matters of country. The Cossacks rebelled, defending the Church and their rights to own property and for self government. Each time during a revolt Poland promised to restore the rights but did not do anything after peace was achieved, transferring monasteries to Unia, introducing Polish Catholic schools and taking away properties from the Orthodox Church. Finally the population of Rus' could take it no more and under the leadership of Bogdan Khmelnitsky, defender of the Cossack rights, Rus' revolted chasing away the Polish-Lithuanian armies. The Southern Rus' requested inclusion with the Muscovite Rus' and after a long time the Czar of Moscow and his Boyar Duma decided to take the Southern Rus' as part of the Muscovite State.

In Lithuanian-Russian territories there was also persecution of the Orthodox people and as result of that, one after another principality went over to the Muscovite State. All the lands of Rus' were included in the Russian state with the exception in the West of Galicia, which was part of Poland and the Carpathian Rus' which became part of the Austro-Hungarian Empire.

In many cities of Rus', churches were built honoring the Mother of God.

Having baptized Rus', the Greeks did not give the Russians the holiday of the Holy Virgin Protection. Being under the yoke of foreign occupation, the Rus' heard from the Greeks that sometime ago the Mother of God came to the church in Czargrad and saved the Greeks from the Saracens. Being under foreign occupation the Russian people and their princes looked for Heavenly protection from the Lord's Mother. Prince Andrew Bogoliubsky called on bishops and it was decided that the Mother of God - is the Heavenly Protector of Rus' and for that reason the holiday of the Holy Virgin Protection was established and Rus' became the Holy Virgin's home. This holiday is celebrated only by the Orthodox people and only in Eastern Europe; neither Catholics nor Protestants celebrate it.

The Mother of God did not leave our forefathers without Her protection and when they called on Her, being surrounded by the Turks in Azov during the siege of the fortress,[85] She came to help

---

[85] * Azov was founded as a Greek colony in the third century B.C., then became a Genoese colony in the 13th century and became subject to Turkey in the middle of 15th century. The Don Cossacks considered that the Turkish fortress there was on their land. In 1637, without the knowlege of the Moscow Czar Michail Feodorovich, the Cossacks under the leader ship of Ataman Talarinow, and with the icon of the Holy Virgin Protection attacked and successfully occupied

them. Five thousand Cossacks and about one thousand Cossack-women were defending the fortress from an army of over two hundred thousand. In the night the defenders of the fortress brought to the wall the Icon of the Holy Virgin Protection and prayed to her leaving themselves to Her mercy. In the morning when it became light, the Cossacks saw that the Turkish army was loaded on their ships and had gone to sea. From that time on all Cossacks began to count the holiday of the Holy Virgin Protection as not only their religious but a Cossack holiday.

Many times later the Russians turned for protection to the Lord's Mother taking with them, on long travel or military expeditions the icon of the Holy Virgin Protection.

The traditions and holidays of our ancestors we do not have the right to forget. Each nation has its own religious and national holidays and costumes and preserving the memory of their ancestors they protect and treasure them.

Our holiday of the Holy Virgin Protection is especially important for us since we came here from far away from our Homeland. It is not easy for our parishioners with difficult work at the woodcutting and flourmill facilities. But the most tragic is that here, in this free country, we do not get the chance and opportunity to believe in God, to celebrate our own holidays and keep our traditions as we did in our Homeland.[86]

Let's all together turn to the Mother of God, putting a candle in front of Her Icon and ask Her to spread her shroud, to help and protect us in our new country. Amen.

Saint Alexis' sermon, given at the church in Old Forge, before the festival Union of the Old Forge parish and its priest to the Orthodox Church.

Brother Russians!

Finally your wish is fulfilled, that about which you have been for more than a year putting forth effort... It is fulfilled after many difficulties and misunderstandings: today you are uniting to your Mother, from which your forefathers were separated by flattery, lies, and force 300 years ago by the enemies of your Mother, by the enemies of the Holy Orthodox Church. Today you are renouncing that one, who put your conscience, on the conscience of your forefathers as an immeasurable yoke, you are renouncing the Pope of Rome, who with his trustworthy slaves, invented the Goddisgusting and besides this also stupid "Unia" which made you free Russian people into disgraceful slaves of Rome and the Pope.[87] You reject this yoke, and again you become as were your forefathers, Orthodox Christians and free Russian people!...

---

the fortress. The Cossacks were there for four years but in 1641 a Turkish army of 200 thousand arrived. The Cossacks fought, without receiving aid from anyone and in the end there were only about 100 warriors and a few women left; all the others were killed or were badly wounded. They prayed to the Holy Virgin Protection icon and brought it to the walls of the fortress. The Turks, having stormed the fortress unsuccessfully 20 times left without taking it, thus sparing the survivors, thanks to the intercession of the Holy Virgin.

[86] *There is a document stating that St. Alexis had even been considering the resettlement of about two thousand families of Carpathians from America to the River Usury in Siberia. His request was sent to the Russian Ambassador to the United States in Washington.

[87] The chief promoters of "Unia" in the Russian territories occupied by Lithuania and Poland, Bishops Cyril Terlelzky and Hipatius Potzey, invented "Unia" with the assistance of Papal Jesuits. They made a secret agreement with Pope Clement VIII because they were afraid that they would be persecuted by the Patriarch of Constantinople for their vicious lives; they thought also that being with the Pope they would obtain protection from the Polish king Sigismund III. They obtained in a deceitful way the signatures of other bishops as if in the name of a Synod and sent it to Rome requesting Unity with Rome (1595). When the clergy and lay people learned about it, it came to a division. As we see Unia came about for selfish ma

Ach! how much can be said about those tortures, about that patience which was carried through your forefathers and fathers through them, from those, who took them from the right way to salvation... but most of you are from Halych, from ageold Russian land, you know not only how to speak Russian, but the majority of you writes and reads Russian: you read and you know how much blood has poured on the Russian land, under the Polish rule, for Christ, for His Holy Orthodox Faith and Church is the only one that brings salvation. I do not want to talk with you about that, you know very well about it as I do also, you know, how those, who forced you into the damned Unia, who were giving your churches, Russian churches for rent to Jews!... It is horrible to think! It was not possible without the Jew either to baptize or to marry, it was not possible even to bury, and even more: the Pascha bread had to be bought from the Jew, without a stamp from the Jew the priest of the Christian Church could not if he did not want to be severely punished, could not bless the Pascha bread! The sanctuary of Christ, the Lord's house, was in Jewish hands!...

I do not wish to talk to you about that man, who indignity of a bishop has been going from place to place with his servants, burning the churches, robbing, church estates, has tortured, killed people... Blood and fire marked his path, wherever he turned with his hordes... Who of you has not heard about "clergy martyr" Josaphat Kuntzevich. [88] Damned is his memory to every Orthodox Russian... However that jerk, that villain, arsonist was made by the "infallible", Pope, the imaginary "Vicar" of Christ a "saint" of the Uniate Church! Only this one saint has the Uniate faith and Church, but that is just the trouble to praise him!...

So "Holy Unia"... across the Russian land by Jews and Kuntzevich, by force, and violence! And the like of that Kuntzevich did not die here either on the free American soil! and here they wished to put through their "twisted truth" by violence, and also to preserve it! Here is an example for you! Yesterday evening a truthful son of "Holy Unia" threw a more than 3 pound rock into the window of the pastor of your souls, and by a hair did not kill him... Only the hand of God saved your spiritual father! And naturally, if this truthful servant of the Pope and of "Holy Unia" would be caught and put into prison probably again he would be made by the Pope if not into a martyr, than at least a "confessor" of Unia.

And what kind of means are they using to put out the rising and increasing Russian Orthodox spirit! They tell that we do not believe in the Holy Trinity, that we do not honor the Mother of God and God knows what else! But what kind "of a truth" is it which they subdue by force, rocks, lies, twisting and blackening of their own brothers. They call us Muscovites... That we are "Muscovites"? What do they understand of this? There is no such nation on earth, but if by the word "Muscovites" they understand a Russian, who loves God and His Holy Orthodox Church, who loves his Russian nationality, who honors loyally, who fulfills God's law, then let's be called

terial purposes, but not for the love of truth and Christian brotherhood . Riots, violence and bloodshed marked the course of "Unia" for centuries, churches and monasteries were de stroyed, sealed and rented to the Jews.

[88] * The Uniate Archbishop Josaphat Kuntzevich of Polotzk, a prelate blindly devoted to the Pope of Rome, persecuted the Orthodox people with particular severity. Leo Sapega, chancellor of Lithuania, strongly warned Kuntzevich of the danger of his conduct in his letter of March 12, 1622!

"...Your sanctity assumes that you are permitted to despoil schismatics and cut off their heads; the Gospel teaches the contrary. The "Unia" has not produced joy, but only discord, quarrels and disturbances. It would have been better if it had never taken place. Now I inform you that, by the King's command, the churches must be opened and restored to the Orthodox, that they may perform divine service. We do not prohibit Jews and Mohametans from having their places of worship, and yet you are closing up Christian temples."

Kuntzevich did not pay attention to this letter pursuing his career of oppression until the inhabitants of Vitebsk rose against him and killed him on July 12, 1628 by throwing him into the river Dvina. The Roman Catholic Church canonized him in 1867 as a saint of the Uniate Church. He became and is until now an obstacle for any agreement between Orthodox and Catholics.

"Muscovites": we will not be ashamed of this name, we will be proud of it and even more than a "Uniate" who is only an imprisoned "schismatic" and it means; that they honor the Pope instead of Christ, that instead of Orthodox Christian teaching, they have some kind of a mixture, which is neither Roman nor Eastern Russian that teaches one to be ashamed of his own nationality and to bow to foreign gods, and to run to one's own enemies, and to suffer from their abuse: then we know what is called "Holy Unia" and what is "schism"... We do not envy this name!... You see here four priests who are offering the bloodless sacrifice, you hear their prayers, you hear their sermons, this is the teaching of the Christian Orthodox Church, this is the teaching of your forefathers, your fathers, this is your faith trough which all of us will come to salvation. Hold to it! Amen.

The Jubilee of the English Queen and our brother Uniates!

He who knows the liberal establishment of the great and glorious Republic of the "United States" and knows its history, would never come to the conclusion, that the citizens of that Republic licked somebody's shoes or that they wish again to be subjects of the English crown! But what do we see? Queen Victoria now celebrates the jubilee of the 60th anniversary of her rule and naturally all the crowned heads of Europe, and nations congratulate her. But the great and free American nation also congratulates the Queen, besides this in churches it also prays for Victoria! All Anglo-Episcopalian churches are filled, and the same prayer, ordained by the leading Bishop of the American-Episcopalian church, Poter, is pronounced and to the mind of no one of the Americans comes the idea to accuse our Episcopalian citizens of treason, and hochverrat! [89] Everybody knows, that even though they have an independent state, the nationality, the faith and the church is common, the same for everybody!...

Czar Peacemaker Alexander III fell asleep; the entire world took part in the greef of the Russian nation, expressing regret and weeping especially the Slavic nations! Only our American Uniates intentionally ignored this event; they did not have a prayer for the repose of the soul, of the pious soul of the great Peacemaker!... Isn't this a shame?.. [90]

The young monarch of Mother Russia Nicholas II was crowned by God; the entire civilized world rejoiced, was glad and congratulated the young monarch. In free America even in non-Orthodox churches this glorious and great event was mentioned, -- only our Uniates were deathly-still,-- they were glorifying the thousandth anniversary of their enslavers, or they were exhaling poisonous saliva on God's anointed, the Russian Emperor because of the unhappy event on Khodynka Field. [91] But this was blood of our blood, flesh of our flesh! The greef and happiness of the great Russian nation -- is our greef, is our happiness! [92]

But no! Not for them; on the burial hills of their ancestors they rejoiced, they were glorifying those who took from them their faith, their fatherland, and stole their nationality!

Isn't it disgraceful, isn't it shameful? Well! Let's assume that it was not possible to do so in the homeland... but who prohibits doing so here on our free unrestricted land... on the land of the American eagle!.. Oh, no! Even here they wished to look for rewards from our federal government and denounced the Orthodox Russians, telling that they are in their prayers mentioning

---

[89] *Hochverral - German - high treason.

[90] *Father Alexis probably did not see the article in ARV, No. 39, 8 November/27 October 1894, pg. 4 in which it is said; "The Czar of All-Russia, the real father of his subjects, the example of state morality and good heartedness, dear father of all wide Russia; the Representative of the Slavic Idea"... "is no longer alive... the flag of the Slavic Idea is lowered to the ground in front of the grave..." However Svoboda expressed no greef at the death of the Czar.

[91] *During the coronation celebration hundreds of people were trampled to death as people rushed to obtain free souvenirs and beer as a result of a rumor that there was not enough for all.

[92] *ARV, No. 21, 11 June 1896, pg 4-5 describes the accident in Moscow at the coronation simply as a tragedy, rather than calling it an evil omen or calling the government unfeeling

the name of the Russian Czar!... They forget this, that the bread of denouncers is the most bitter! They write home and they ask for a biskup, among other "arguments?!" They also write and say that the Russians from Hungary and Galicia, returning to the faith of their ancestors the Holy Orthodox Church, pray for the Russian Czar ("Muscovite" literally)!... Uniate ksendzes saw their hochverrat, the printed calendar of the "Union" for the year 1897 had a photograph of the Russian Czar; they stopped sending it out and selling it!...

Until what time will you brother-Uniates fool and blind yourselves and your nation? Until what time will you stick out your necks for your enemies? And when finally will the grace of the Holy Ghost fill your hearts and your minds, that you will not be ashamed of the Russian name and your real mother the Holy Orthodox Church! Is it not that you live in America, in that America, whose cornerstone is: the free conscience!...

You should learn now from the Anglo-Americans who pray for that Queen with whom politically they have nothing in common, they pray for her and they bring their prayers to God! By nationality she is English, by faith Episcopalian. When will it be possible also to say the same thing about our Russian Uniates? Indeed the faith and nationality of the great glorious Russian nation -- this is our faith, our nationality!...

ORGANIC DECOMPOSITION

CHAPTER I

The condition of the Uniates in their church at the present time has come to that level.- or it would be better to say, has fallen to such a degree, at which it starts to decompose, to rot and to deteriorate,- in medical language doctors call it - desssolutio organica.

Really this condition is deplorable, extremely deplorable, and it could not even be different because of the subject of the matter,- the illfated Uniates. Unia - is an illegitimate and prematurely born child of the Roman Church, as a matter of fact - of the Roman Pope, and of several traitors of the Russian nation; it was born with no life in it and it was fed only by persecutions, bloodshed and prisons, so that in three hundred years it could hardly grow - it could have survived only by all kinds of treatment, that a German calls "Kurpfuscherei", [93] not by natural means,- it became a cripple and this is not its own soul, this was not inborn, not organic, and came only as a loan from the Roman Church; because of that this cripple - Unia is such a monster, here in America, that its lawful father - the Roman Pope does not want to acknowledge it as his own child, and its nurses and nurturers see for themselves, that here with such means it is not possible to support it, with that which supported it in old decrepit Poland, - and with which, it is partially, supported today in Galicia and Hungary. And here also began its horrible failure,- and all kinds of "folk" medicine was invented, such as Congresses and Memorandums, so to keep up at least for a time the mechanical life of the cripple. It is not known, whether it was by some casual circumstance, or if it was intentional but just at the time in the socialistic newspaper "Svoboda", that leans toward the Poles,- Count Leliva - according to the pseudonym a Pole or a Lithuanian, but in reality a Russian, is trying to prove, that "Unia" - was not a political Jesuistic trick, but was purely a religious matter, and as a matter of fact he proves (?) it from such a standpoint, that it is hard to believe, that this gentleman knows anything of the history of that church, to which he belongs? And in the Uniates' "Amerikanskii-Russkii Viestnik" Mr. Orlov - probably also a pseudonym, - under the title "Our Church Business" brings up Jeremiah-like complaints and in one of them (issue no. 47-4) he says naively "... and by whom in the Old Country have we been convinced that the reduction in the rules and laws of our church was a matter which was conducted by politics..." In other words this glorious author wants to convince not only himself but also wants to convince other people, that the illfated Unia was not brought about by politics, was created by sincere religious will,- and meanwhile here in America it turned out, that politics does not have anything to do with the church, and namely it does not have any

---

[93] * "Kurpfuscherei" - German - cure bungling; to do a bad job of the cure.

business whatsoever with the Uniate Church, does not support it, and because of this the mechanical life of "Unia" begins to die and - organic decomposition starts! - In Poland, in Galicia, in Hungary there are only political goals to destroy the Russian nationality - these are the reasons that Unia is supported,- since with it you would take away from a Russian the Orthodox faith, and you would force him into another one, - in this case into the Latin one, - his spirit and consciousness would be taken also, and he would begin to be ashamed of his nationality and he would become a Polack and a Hungarian! This has been proved by fact: thousands of people in Poland became Poles, in Hungary - Hungarians, only because of one reason, because they ended on the religious bridge - Unia, and came over to Latinization, and simultaneously they ceased to be Russians!

We will not speak about "Count" Leliva, because his work is not yet finished, - we will wait until it is finished, and then we will talk, but now we will look over the philosophizing of the writer Orlov in his article: "Our Church Business" - mostly in the 4 th article (ARV, No.47), where we can find a very sincere confession at first and secondly Mr. Orlov continuously fights with healthy reason and logic, but in none of his philosophizing does he put logic upside down so much, as he does in the 4 th article, and he does not become as much inconsequent as in this one.

Until now we were used to the "great speeches" of "Amerikanskii-Russkii Viestnik", about "our dear Union" - about "our lawful priests", about "our fortyfive churches", about the "splendid blessings" of the "cornerstones", - about drums, music, parades, marches, about "loudly pronounced sermons", then about "itinerant disciples", about "schismatics' promises", about "witnessless attacks", etc., etc. - and these have been the usual subjects of "our dear organ"! Show could it have happened that "our organ" at this time began sad Jeremiahlike complaints about - the "troubled conditions of church business" to write it in a simple way,- this can be asked plainly with surprise! - and even better,- in a very decent way it poured cold water over the "vicarship" and the candidate for bishop Nicephor Chanath himself!... This confession is a very nice one; now everybody can see, that the rotting and nudity cannot be covered up with music, tambourines, parade marches! But Amerikanskii-Russkii Viestnik would not be a Viestnik, [94] if it would be consequent. It confesses, - but doesn't seek repentance! It shows clearly, that that road, which was until now taken by the Uniates, brought them into an unbridgeable gulf and distraction, that Rome and Unia are the reasons for all of their misfortunes,- but however, it is too weak, to say frankly, courageously; - "Let's stop! Let's return to our original road, let's go again to our Mother Orthodox Church, she cares not only about our souls but also preserves our Russian nationality... There was enough calamity, there has been enough disdain, there has been enough lackeys and servility, - our biskups don't care about us, - only about their own problems; Rome is destroying us, subjecting us to the local Catholic biskups, who take away from us churches, nationality, rite, who take away our rights, keep us slaves, who do injustice to us, who want to tear us away from the church, the nationality; and our ksendzes are only filling their pockets, sending the money to Hungarian banks, and doing nothing about the nation, about the churches and about the schools,- let's go back there where our beloved Mother Orthodox Church is who cares about her children, who cares about them sincerely and with love..., let's be Russians, let's be again sons, as our fathers and forefathers were: you know in us there is Russian blood flowing,- we have the right to live in the same way, as other nations, you know that the faith is ours, the church has been given by Christ the Saviour, by that faith and in that church our fathers and forefathers have saved themselves: - they were glorious and courageous, until the time that they fell away from the faith, from the church, and accepted Unia! Everybody honored them, as they also honor those Russians, who today keep the forefathers' Orthodox faith!..."

No!... Mr. Orlov does not do it, but with emphasis he says, that the Uniates must: "with greater energy rise to the protection of their church rites and laws, and the sooner the better with full strength".. But against whom? Or what? Is it against "schismatics", the Orthodox?... No... God protect!.. The Orthodox are today no longer their enemies!.. But against Catholic biskup, against Rome, against "our old country bishops", who according to the words of Mr. Orlov, "not to lose the greatest kindness and gratitude, they themselves help gradually to shorten the rites and laws of the Greek Catholic Church and of the Eastern rite..." Indeed, staggering sincerity from the "organ", which until now glorified to the sky Rome, and Catholic biskups, and "our old country bishops"! - especially the sincerity is staggering, because until now the Uniates accepted

---

[94] * A pun - viestnik means messenger

the local Catholic biskups not only with tambourines, drums, music, but allowed their churches to be registered in their names, took jurisdiction from them, ran to them for protection, for defense against "schismatics", - accepted and acknowledged them as their archpastors, and exactly now the official organ shows them as the greatest enemies of the Greek Catholic Church and of Eastern rite?... Nun sagt mir graf Orlov-Orindur waher dieser zwiespall der natur?..[95] We ask you... Did you just now become conscious of this? You know it was already told to you and to the Uniates for 6-7 years, and it was forecast that the Uniate Church will fall so deep, if you by force throw yourself into the arms of the local Catholic biskups!.. And what has your official "organ" been doing? Blackening and attacking everyone who said what it today says! Funny logic! Earlier for him the "schismatics" were the greatest enemies, and today he selflessly acknowledges, that:

"....we already know and are convinced that, the greatest enemies
of our faith and rite are not anymore - schismatics... but the greatest
and most dangerous enemy of our faith, rite, church rights, laws,
nationality and language is the American Roman Catholic hierarchy,-
where under the raincoat of Catholicism is the hidden and all ab-
sorbing Irish aspiration for power, whose influence is also favored
by Rome"! (No. 47, pg. 2)

Wonderful!... This confession moves one to tears!... But if the matter stands like that, then why is Mr. Orlov, who stepped on the road of repentance, fooling again himself and others, acknowledging, that Orthodoxy is not the enemy of the Russian nationality nor of the Eastern rite, nor of the church - and has never been; as you know the foundation of Orthodoxy is: to keep true Christian teaching, to support the Holy Eastern Rite,- the Eastern Catholic or it would be better to say the Ecumenical church, to support the Russian nationality - especially here in America; - no,... Mr. Orlov, and the official "Viestnik" would not be Viestnik, if it would be consequent. To him the Orthodox or according to his fanatical terminology, taken from the Papists, the "schismatics" are therefore not enemies: "because all their kinds of intrigue, rebellion and fraud, all kinds of misleading promises - did not disturb in our nation love and devotion to its faith and rite... The leaders of the 'schism' among our people had no moral meaning, nor authority!"... Those words show extreme hate!- "Amerikanskii-Russkii Viestnik" constantly trumpets about "intrigues", "rebellions" and "frauds" but until now not even once did it prove all that with specific facts... All this is naked - and idletalk has been and will be forever; as the head so are the words! [96] And to that concerning "love of the people for the faith and rite" - to that we say: Orthodoxy would have spread such meanness and darkness, as Unia, if it would have fought against the faith and against the rite.- What kind of special "Eastern rite" do the Uniates have? that wasn't taken from the Orthodox Church? Don't the Uniates have the rite, that the Holy Apostles, the Holy Ecumenical Councils, the Holy Fathers, namely: St. Basil the Great, Saint John Chrysostom, Saint John of Damascus and others gave to the Holy Eastern Orthodox Church; hasn't it been the same rite that was promised to you by pans when your Judas and traitors of the Christian faith: Tertetsky, Potzey and others denounced Orthodoxy,- if you acknowledge him, [97] and not Christ, as the head of the church? and the same pans and their puppet biskups are today taking it away from you, and they already partially took it! Then why is Mr. Orlov complaining, that the Catholic biskups and Rome are the greatest enemies not only of the Greek Catholic Church but also of the Eastern rite! And where is the Eastern Church rite kept unharmed: by you? Is that Eastern rite - to perform two, even three masses in one day? Or to whisper the masses is that also Eastern rite? To perform the Liturgy without the Proskomide [98] is that also Eastern rite? Not to glorify the Nine [99] and the Proskomide, or to hold the service with "wafers",... to introduce or-

---

[95] "Nun sagt... - German - "Now tell me Count Orlov-Orindur from where comes this splintering of nature?"

[96] * as the head... - a Russian proverb.

[97] "Father Alexis is referring to the Pope of Rome.

[98] "Proskomide - Greek - to bring an offering. It is the first part of the Divine Liturgy.

[99] "The Nine - Particles from file prosphora (loaves) are prepared during the Divine Liturgy, in token

gans in churches, to throw out of the church the iconostasis,[100] to bless in ovens the Pascha bread, to perform the Liturgy in the basements of the Papists' kostels, on "peace to all" to spread apart the hands, to let Catholic biskups or their representatives "bless" the Uniate churches etc. , etc. Is this - Eastern rite? Say it for God's sake! Who of the Holy Fathers ordered this to the Orthodox Church? The attitude toward the "rite" you people call "love"? You call that "Eastern rite"? Don't fool yourself - and uneducated people too! Against such kind of "Eastern rite" naturally the Ecumenical church and namely the Eastern Orthodox - always rises and will not allow such abuses to be held as "Eastern rite". - But if you keep to them, then at least say frankly, that this is "our special Uniate rite" but don't say that it is Eastern, - you know, that the Eastern rite is kept clearly, solidly and not falsely only in the Holy Orthodox Church, and not in the Uniate! Concerning "meaning" and "authority" we will say, that the leaders of Orthodoxy have the respect and authority not only of "their" people, but also the Eastern Orthodox - "heterodoxes" we can show it by facts, - "their own" honor them so much, that until now not even one Orthodox "leader", that is priest, has been thrown out of the church by his parishioners, not even one has been thrown down the stairs; they don't have to go under police protection to church nor do they have to go fearfully from the church carrying in their hands the "Holy Eucharist", so that the people won't beat them up; they are not forced to move almost every two month from one parish to another; it is known that among the Uniate leaders there are such, who during six years were in seven parishes but not even one of the Orthodox "leaders" goes into the parish of another one as the Uniates do, to rebel and to stir up the people, promising to serve for a "thinner" contribution and collection: all these and other facts are the bright proof of the "meaning", "respect", and "authority" of the Uniate leaders! If Mr. Orlov or somebody else wishes, we will give him not only the facts, but with full pleasure also the names. No,- Mr. Orlov, if you acknowledge one part of the matter, that Orthodoxy is not - and never has been the enemy of the Russian people and of the Eastern rite, then you also have to acknowledge the other part with selflessness, and not quote absurd tirades from "Viestnik" about "promises", "intrigues", "frauds", but say courageously Orthodoxy is the only protection of our church, of our Russian nationality, of our Eastern rite... All this is clearly shown by these facts, that Orthodoxy, in spite of our slanders, lies, cheats, trials, and ugly attacks, with every day strengthens and spreads and where the Russians are enlightened by the Holy Spirit, and where they have their churches and parishes, there is peace, and quiet.. And if there is not quietness, then we - the Uniates and our "most beloved pans" are doing it for our profits and pockets! - so let us also go there, and then we will not be overpowered, neither by Irish biskups, nor by Rome and then there will be peace upon us - harmony and God's grace. Do it and then you will find success! Otherwise you will perish in the Papal Sea forever... in what way? We will tell you frankly, listen!...

---

of the miraculous feeding of fife thousand people by Christ. The first prosphora represents Christ. It is the only one that is prepared for the sacrament of the Eucharist. A portion of the second prosphora is taken in memory of the Virgin Mary. Nine particles are taken from the third prosphora in commemoration of the nine ranks of glorified saints: 1) the Forerunner, 2) the Prophets, 3) the Apostles, 4) the Hierarchies, 5) the Martyrs, 6) the Chaste, 7) the Unmercenaries, 8) Joachim and Anna and the saints who are being commemorated on the day the Liturgy is being celebrated, 9) in honor of the originator of the Liturgy being performed. Particles taken from the fourth loaf are for the health and salvation of the living and particles from the fifth prosphora are for the remission of sins of the dead.

[100] "Iconostasis - The image-screen. The high wall covered with sacred pictures that divides the sanctuary from the nave of the church. The icons are placed there in a prescribed order. The iconostasis has 3 doors - the middle double doors are called the Royal Doors (or Holy Gates) - the clergy comes through them carrying the Chalice (Communion Cup) with Christ Himself the Host. The four evangelists, Matthew, Mark, Luke and John are portrayed on icons on the Royal Doors surrounding the center icon which portrays the Annunciation. An icon portraying the Last Supper, where the sacrament of Communion was instituted by Christ, is placed above the Royal Doors; to the right of the Royal Doors is the icon of the Lord Jesus Christ and to the left an icon of Mary, the Mother of God To the right of the icon of Christ is placed an icon representing the saint or sacred event for which the church is named and to whom the church building is dedicated. Some churches have as many as five tiers of icons on the iconostasis. In its entirety, the iconostasis presents a great panorama of the founders and builders of the Christian Church including both the Old and New Testaments

CHAPTER II

I assume, that you know something of the history of the Russian people in Hungary, you know what the Papists have done and are doing now under the pretext of Catholicism and of taking the "greatest care" of the Russian Uniates, you know, that violence has been that Christian Apostolic means, which was used by your benefactors,- also by the first killer Josaphat, [101] who spread Unia among the Russians: you know, how much labor, how much despite and how much money has been used, before the Pope canonized the diocese of Mukachevo in Hungary and took it from the claws of the Bishop of Eger, - you know, what is happening today in Galicia, that the Pope takes the monasteries from the Russians; that he enforces celibacy, that he wants to implant there the Roman rite; you know, that your counts, biskups do not dare for your protection say even a word in Rome: here in America you see all that falsehood, done by the Catholic biskups, who today persecute by not completely visible means, using secret means they instruct to be registered in their names the churches build by the horny hands of the poor Russian people; that today the entrance to America is strictly prohibited to married Uniate clergy, you see the horrible disorder in your parishes; people quarreling with their spiritual fathers, chasing them away,- in many places they even renounce Unia, and they go to the Catholic kostels, accepting the Latin Papacy, you know the history of your "Memorandums" for the period of the last eight years, you know the comedy - which is tragically sad about the election of a Uniate "vicar", [102] you know the apostolic deeds of the "Vicar" and some of your greatly respected "pans", you know, to get a "biskup", your people every year create new plans, you see and you acknowledge, that today you and your Uniate church, faith, and rite are at the edge of extinction, you acknowledge yourself, that your greatest enemies are - the local Catholic biskups, [103] but you still accept, the same politic; harmful to you, threatening you with extinction and moral death which Rome supports under the pretext of taking the greatest care of you, and your "old country bishops" are helping Rome and the Irish biskups... you even tranquilly admit, that Rome, that is the Pope, the head of your church, is your greatest enemy, he who ordered the local biskups to swallow you here, to wipe you out, and to take you from the Russian nation, to take away from you your rite, and to make out of you Latin Papists!...

You, Mr. Orlov and the Uniates want to protect yourselves against such meanness; and you do not want to let yourself and your church, your nationality, and your rite become extinct, isn't it true? Well! But how do you want to save yourselves? By Memorandums and by sending delegations to Washington, to Priashev, to Uzgorod, even to Rome? To the same Rome, which is according to your words, your greatest enemy, to those biskups, who do not do anything in any way for you... say it in the Lord's name! Where here is reason, where logic? You do it in the same way as if a sheep would go with a complaint to a wolf or to a bear, would get into his dwelling- burrow - to complain to him about him, that he ate its lamb! Tell me, when has Rome been your sincere father, when did it sincerely want, the Uniate Church to blossom? From the beginning Rome worked and it works also today to bring you over that bridge, called "Unia" to the Latin Papacy: how very blind you are Mr. Orlov and all Uniates, that you do not want to see these facts?... The matter would be very laughable,- if it weren't so sad... to go with a complaint to Rome against Rome, to complain to the Pope, against the Papacy!... You probably even believe still in that empty sentence: appelare a pontifice ad nelius informandum pontificem- tell me how many bulls, orders, and other insignificant papers have been given by Popes; Clement, Urban VIII,

---

[101] * Josaphat (Kuntzevich) of Polotsk. See footnote in Father Alexis' "Sermon at Old Forge".

[102] * See ARV, No. 29, 21-9 August, 1894, pg. 1.

[103] * ARV, No. 17, 26 April - 8 May, 1894, pg. 2.
"...bishops of Latin rite to whom we are directed, do not know our rites, our rights, they do not have even the slightest good wishes for our national church goals and therefore can't rule over us and represent our interests. . only our bishop can and divisions..." ARV, No. 17, 16 May, 1895, pg. 2.
"... It is necessary for the Uniates to have here our own bishop, without whom people join the schism... but publicly we can say, that the reason for this is not Muscovism, not rubles, not doubts in Catholicism, but especially the local Latin rite bishops and ksendzes... Whose fault is it? That of the Apostolic See"

Benedict XIV, (among which the most important is: Allalae sunt), Gregory XVI, Pius IX, and Leo XIII and others for the "benefit" of the Uniate Church, and who fulfills them? the Catholic biskups? It is obvious, what is happening in Galicia, and in Hungary, and with you here in America!... And you want to send a delegation to Rome with a "Memorandum"?... How many of those "Memorandums" have been sent everywhere?.. And what kind of a result is there from them? You know very well, and you even fear, that this "Memorandum" will be simply put ad acta! And that's how the matter will be, and I will frankly tell it to you, and for this you do not have to have high education, nor prophetic talents. The reasons are as follows:

1) How can cooperation logically be expected from those Irish biskups, who at the time when the first Uniate priest appeared here, made such outcry even though he is like a Catholic Uniate, but that he is of a different rite, not Latin, but Greek Eastern, and consequently, such rite, that they from there began hating us, because in their opinion the rite is "heretical", "schismatic", [104] and later they didn't want even to accept all arriving Uniate priests, and if they accepted them then they did it with the pride of sovereigns, in order to throw them then out of the room, later some of them were damned by them, proclaimed as unlawful priests, and today they also do not want to acknowledge the married clergy, constantly they demand of Rome that the "Greeks" (that is the Uniate priests) would be recalled. Really you have to be a naive Uniate to believe, that Rome will give you a special Uniate biskup, that Unia will be supported here and that two rites of the Papal Church will be spread here! The local biskups would never agree to that and the Pope with all his infallibility, and with all his primacy will not do anything because he does not want to lose their "kindness" and "favor". At the present time only America or better to say the American Papists support the constantly empty treasury of the Roman Pope - "the mite of St. Peter" is the richest in America! Then, in Rome the local bishops are anyhow suspect, that some of them are too liberal and are dreaming about a national American church. Already the circumstance, that the Irish occupy with a slight exception, all Catholic biskups' cathedra and in the parishes there are in the majority Irish - ksendzes can convince the Uniates of the infeasibility of their wishes. The Irish, concerning fanaticism and Papacy is a second Polack; if not worse: and for him he who is not Irish, and who is not a Catholic, is not even a human being! But even that they agree with the Polacks in the main points of Catholicism, the Irish biskups do not want to hear the idea, that there would be a Catholic biskup - of the Polish nationality! And you know that there are here 2.5 million Polacks! The Irish have founded a monopoly for themselves here! And now let's take in comparison with the Polacks a handful of the Uniates who are besides everything of a different rite,- how can it be even dreamed by a poor Uniate to get his own biskup?

2) Moreover, Cardinal Simeoni in his instruction of 1889 said clearly, that the local biskups should not allow "unity of the faith" to be broken by introducing here into the Catholic Church two rites. Then Cardinal Satolli, the former Papal delegate, in 1896, to the demand of the Uniates about their own biskup announced "If you, Uniates, are loyal sons of the Apostolic See, that is Rome, then you have to obey also its commands, and it was ordered to you to obey the local Catholic biskups". In 1895, when Orthodoxy so quickly spread here, the Papal delegates, to keep in Unia the Uniate representatives, that is their ksendzes were allowed to perform a funny comedy to elect for themselves a "Vicar"! Those poor people did not foresee that this was only a foolish trick... they elected for themselves with a majority of voices - whom? Nicephor Chanath! But the matter also stopped there: the Vicar was not affirmed either by the delegates, or by the Pope. Neither was he "ordained", - unless he did it himself... the poor fellow temporarily acted the part of a Vicar, but when he saw, that even his closest friends and his "loyal herd" made fun of him in spite of that, he ordered made for himself a robe with violet buttons and with exultation ordered himself called "great lord", he remained only in Scranton, and he, the "Vicar" last summer had to go to the church under the protection of a policeman and finally, now in addition the official Uniate organ "Viestnik" poured cold water over him,- afterward he officially renounced that "great" position, but privately he still counts himself as a "Vicar", and dreams that he will be affirmed by

---

[104] * Svoboda, 1904, No. 21. Rev. N. Dmitrov writes about Uniates in America that already in 1884, when the first Rusin Uniate priest, Father John Volansky, came and met Archbishop Patrick Ryan of Philadelphia, Archbishop Ryan learning that Father John was married ordered his Irish, Polish and Lithuanian Latin rite priests to condemn Father John from their pulpits. This was the first sign of Latin intolerance toward the Uniates in the United States as Rev. Dmitrov said.

Rome, that is that the Pope will affirm him in the order of a biskup... the more so, that one Catholic biskup supports him, until the time when the entire Uniate matter will not completely compromise here...

In short, let the convention, "Viestnik" and Mr. Orlov make up as much as they want of projects, plans, Memorandums and all kinds of inventions,- the matter will still remain: in America there will never be a Uniate biskup! The greatest enemies of the Uniates are Rome and the Catholic biskups who oppose them!

3) Pato non concesso,- let's assume that the local biskups and Rome would agree to the presence of a Uniate biskup here, and what will happen then? That, only a maximum of ten Uniate ksendzes will accept him, the majority will not, because, among local Uniate ksendzes there are disagreements, hate, hostility increased to an unprecedented level. The Uniate Russian ksendzes from Hungary hate the Galicians and call them Polacks,- the Galicians in their turn call the former Hungarians, the ksendzes from the Priashev diocese dislike those from Mukachevo and the latter hate those from Priashev, then,- among the majority of the ksendzes from Galicia there is the smell of socialism,- their organ "Svoboda" proves it in the best way, besides this they dream more about uniting their nation and the "creation" of the "Ukraine" then about the biskup. So whose and for whom will there be a biskup? The most important matter, who is going to support him? The people? Well! But as a matter of fact these people today do not want to pay their ksendzes, and the biskup will have to go then with the "collection plate" himself for a collection. But enough about a biskup.

Now to the question, what will happen to "Unia" in its present condition? Unia, as has been said above, and as every man with a healthy mind can determine is a politically Jesuitical undertaking, it is a tree without roots, it is a prematurely born baby, it is a cripple! It can exist only there where the government is supporting it for political goals; and as soon as this support stops, that is, as soon as the state and the government will not care about Unia,- as can be judged according to what is happening in America - organic decomposition starts, decay, decline, finally deterioration and complete death!...

The destiny of the Uniates is very determined and anyone can foresee its end, those in whose veins still runs Russian blood, and whose hearts and spirits are Russian, will return to their beloved mother, the Holy Orthodox Church; those, to whom it has been enough dimmed into their heads, that the "Greek and Roman" faiths are "the same", for whom the Papal indulgences, the organs, and other Latin traditions are dear, those are lost and by their nationality, they cease to be Russian and they will become completely Latin Papists! They are a minority,- and another, the least significant minority will leave the faith, the Church, and the nationality and they will become socialist radicals. Such will be the fate of "Holy Unia" - because, it was said: "male parta male dilabuntur", every matter, for which there was not God's blessing will perish, and for Unia there was not only no blessing, but there was damnation, weapons, tortures, prisons, killings... The innocent blood screams to the sky,- and Unia has to perish!

Let's speak seriously

In a "small topical satire" in the newspaper "Svoboda" number 6, signed by Spectator, were some compliments. As he stated: "Archpriest A. Toth has written not a bad article in the "Amerikanskii Pravoslavnyi Viestnik" named "Organic decomposition". We have to agree that in certain points his thoughts are full of wisdom but in general this person expressed strong and detailed interest in church matters in America.." Up to this point it sounds like a compliment... which must be a big concession from "Svoboda" mainly because the Spectator expresses (extripode) his ideas independently and even acknowledges, that "this person expresses strong interest in church matters in America".

Thanks to God! Finally, after 9 years, the Spectator has made a discovery about this person, but to tell the truth "this person" even before this discovery had "expressed strong and detailed interest" in those church matters, and has never been occupied with other matters; for example he has not involved with the sale of oysters or boots!... However such a compliment remains a compliment, and "this person" if his memory does not fool him, has been honored by "Svoboda" for the second time with the greatest praise!... What can be done? Naturally, we have to say thanks!

But it is not to the Spectator's taste, that "that person" has connected and related all disturbances and all disagreements, and all absurdities and disorders to the illfated Unia; and namely here in America among the Russian people. He calls that a "crafty trick of "that person's message"!...

According to the opinion of the Spectator - that is "absolutely a soap bubble" because "Unia is a Unia outside by itself and Orthodoxy is also by itself, and the Roman Catholics are by themselves Catholics." That is a genius interpretation! but since "that person" understands the matter, then he expresses even more than he wishes: and that is that a Russian person can be a good Russian - if he is a Uniate, or an Orthodox or a Roman Catholic; therefore, why not Jewish? Then it would be completely according to the Polish principle: Polack Roman, Polack Eastern, Polack of any other denomination is always a Polack, in other words the religion does not have anything to do there. If the Spectator wished to speak frankly, then he should have said that, - and not that the Unia has here "nothing to do!" - There is no cunning necessary here or any kind of ingenuity. A Russian is only then a Russian, if he has his faith. This faith is Orthodox; otherwise he is not a Russian anymore! Tertium non datur! He will become a Greek-Catholic. (That is a nationality per eminentiam of Ugro-Russians, who are ashamed of their own nationality and who have for themselves invented the "Hreko-Kaftoliezeskuyu" nationality. The main place where this nationality has its ruling body is here in America.- That is "our dear Union" - and its gospel was written in the Jucatan-Ostrogoth "peoples" language" - by "our dear organ of the press". Its faith is - "our common interests". And what are the results: Russkii, Rus'kii, Ruthenian written according to the Polish grammatical rules and all kind of radical fantastic-dreams, socialist foolishness, visions about an "independent nation", and about the "Ukraine". The conjurer of this nation is here in the Mount-Carmel newspaper "Svoboda" and its apostles have not had time to bring "the only saving catechism" from Galicia. But they brought here some basics of Franko's faith and nationality. [105] Thanks to the teachings of these "ksendz-patriots" who were educated in the time of Cardinal Sembratowicz and who were sent here to America for the "enlightenment" of the people, those ideas began to spread here also.

The Orthodox Faith - that is the spirit of the Russian person! For what have Russians in Old Poland been persecuted? Why are they also now persecuted in Galicia and in Hungary? Why did it happen at the last metropolitan council in Lvov that all the resolutions that were made introduced more of the Papal teaching for the Galician-Russian people! [106] Was that done to more easily

---

[105] "Franko, Ivan Iakovlevich, (1856-1916). A Western Ukrainian writer, poet, critic and activist He was born in a farm family, studied in the Universities of Lvov and Vienna and propagandized the ideas of Russian- Revolutionary Democracy and then Marxism.

[106] * See "Katolische Kirchenzeitung Salzburg", 1 5, 1898

save the souls of these people? No! That was done with the intention of killing the Russian national feelings among these people! If you succeed in convincing the Hungarian or Galician-Russian that it is the "same faith" to be Roman or to be Greek-Catholic, then these people will also look at their nationality as if it is wszystko jedno (Polish - meaning 'the same') "to be a Rusin or Polak". And there is even more since some patriots dream that "Polszcza, Rus' i Litwa have to have the same faith!" Is it therefore a miracle that a "Rusin yokel" begins to join the Poles, to visit the Polish coscioly (Catholic churches), to chant at "jubileuszach polskich" (Polish celebrations), to take part, especially, if he sees that His Greatness is present as a delegate representing the Russians, at the Polish "sejmie" (convention) ... and then that person is lost for the Russian Church, and to the nationality! Facta loguuntur!

Unia teaches the principle of "wszystko jedno" - and by doing that, it destroys the Rusins' faith and nationality - Orthodoxy however teaches: "keep your faith - and by doing that you will save not only your soul, but will preserve also your nation!" The Serbians who have accepted Roman Catholicism now call themselves "Croatians". But their language is today the same as that of the Serbians; they call themselves also "Bunevaz", but not Serbians! The Russians, who accepted Unia, compose now the "Greek-Catholic" - "Ruthenian" Ukrainian nationality, and as the Roman Catholic Croatians are hostile to the Orthodox Serbians, so also the Uniates do not wish to acknowledge that the Great Russians are their brothers; no, they say they are "moscovites"... and we are an "independent nation". Why do they do something like that? - Because the Poles in Europe, and "Svoboda" from Mt. Carmel in America teach them that!...

Where the Orthodox Faith is, there also is the National Church... Can the "Specta-tor" therefore tell that in Germany there is a "National German Roman-Catholic Church" or is there a French or Italian? Though what is their Church nationality? Isn't it that their Church services are in Latin, and therefore in a language foreign for them; and also that is now dead? Does the Roman Church permit even in principle to have a national church? Why did it fight so hard against the idea of Gallicanism? [107] Finally, why is it then that the Uniate Church from year to year introduces more and more Papal inventions and traditions? Why does "the national" (at least it looks naturally as if it is national) color of Unia have to be destroyed, and its members brought into the circle, where there is Papism with its mechanical, unnatural, and not internal union!

Orthodoxy teaches and preserves the nationality! Catholicism - preaches cosmopolitanism; its goal is to preserve the domination of the Pope! Unia is a very small planet of Papism, and it is being attracted by the greater mass of Roman Catholicism where it is going to be drowned, together with the nationality of people in Unia!... it will happen sooner or later, but it will be drowned and then Unia will be gone!

Unia has spread discord, disturbances even the shedding of blood in Russian lands, there where it was under the rule of Poland.- It made people morally wild, brought hate and killings, and has lowered moral standards, since people look to their pastors as examples. The fanatism among these people has been developed and has increased up to the limit. This is an historical truth, that everyone, who has even read once the history of the Russian people, knows. Unia has brought here among the Russians in America the same discord, disturbances, disagreements and court trials!

The "Spectator" said: "the main reason for our contemporary church disturbances are the grabby greediness and the ignorance of priests, who were called here as first Apostles to the churches in America. Look for example at Freeland..."

Speaking of that "grabby greediness", since the Spectator brought up this dear characteristic, there is no necessity "to look" at Freeland. That "grabby greediness" has a much longer his-

---

[107] * Gallicanism is a complex of theological doctrines and political positions according to which a church can be independent of the Papacy of Rome and the king. The leaders of the Roman Catholic Church in France, after a long study of that theory, concluded that the Resolutions of the Ecumenical Councils were of higher authority than those of the Roman Popes. They pronounced that all bishops of the Church were of divine institution. They also believed that as citizens of a state, the members of the Church organization can ask state assistance in cases of financial and disciplinary problems. The Gallicanist ideas can be traced in France as far back as the 14th century, but their influence peaked in the 17th and 18th centuries These ideals were approved in 1682 by King Louis XIV in the so-called "Four Articles" which in ef fect proclaimed a concept of an independent French Catholic Church.

lory. A great "grabby greediness" was demonstrated by the first Uniate apostle in America, I.V., who registered the churches, which were built by the Russian workers in Shenandoah, Kingston and Hazleton, in his own and his wife's names as their property, and before he left, returning to the Old Country, he gave the deeds to his successor, the notorious A. plene jure et cum beneficio inventurii! And what did this latter one do with them? He decided on his own to sell all the church deeds at an auction, and afterward he also left America. Before that, he was considered a national "patriot" by the "Russkoe Slovo", in which he wrote articles about the blossoming of the working people. In other words he was a devoted son of the new Galician time, and he definitely belongs there. At the time of the disturbances made by A., "this person" about whom "Svoboda" said that he was still "a greenhorn" also came to America. He very soon understood the local conditions, as the Spectator would have called them in "one hundred days"! He did not like many things, especially, that the Irish biskup also our brothers - the Polish ksendzes treated the Uniates "very badly", like animals. And then "that person" called all fellow priests to come to Wilkes-Barre to have a discussion. Everyone came there, with the exception of Rev. Frs. Gulovich and Andrukhovych. The latter was even making fun of the "ecumenical council". The priests that met wrote about their bitter experience to their bishops; namely to Lvov, Ungvar (Uzhorod) and Presov. And that was where it was found out how much Holy Unia really meant?! The bishops from Presov and Mukacevo sent their petitions to Rome. The bishop from Lvov did not do anything, - he was by then already dreaming of a "cardinal's hat", and he did well, since Simeon, the Prefect of the Propagation of the Faith, in Rome - did not defend the rights of Unia, but even officially declared that it is a small matter. He gave to the local bishops in America such instructions and means, that the American Uniate Church has been brought to its present condition. If the Pope and his satellites had paid as much attention to Unia, as the Uniates imagine they do, they would not have let the matter go so far. But since Unia was only planned as a "bridge" in the road to a full acceptance of Papism; and since the government here in America does not support any particular religion, - and does not use them in its politics either, as is the case in Austria; Unia therefore is left to itself. As the matter stands, the strong and mighty Papacy is pretending to protect, but in reality it has swallowed up Unia, and also the nationality of people that are Uniates. No, Pan (Mr.) Spectator, the priests' "lack of awareness" was not completely the reason for that sad condition, but Unia itself and its Highest Protector - the Infallible Vice-God of Rome! And Spectator's references to the Russians are in vain. Like the Galicians, the Hungarian Russians were always convinced that they were Orthodox; but since you refuse to tell these people, here in a free country, - and as before their spiritual pastors do not admit, - that they are no longer Orthodox, but Uniate, then there was no necessity to put these people voluntarily through such contempt and humiliation.   There was no reason to write all these "memorandums" and humble requests from Saul to Paul, from Pontius Pilatus for their "own biscup" here in America, since there had already been for 100 years a Russian Orthodox Eminence and Bishop here. Then why did all the Uniate priests in corpore not turn to him? especially, when "this person" without any ulterior motive in 1892 called on them to do that. Why did they then, if really the interests of the Russian people are so dear to their hearts, - not accept his word, but in the name of their "councils" did send their memorandums to Cardinal Gibbon, to Rome and to God knows where else. They wrote denunciations, requests for a biscup, and pointed to the threat of schism and "Muscovite Rubles" as the main reason to have him here!... If at that time all of them would have done what "that person" did, - where would we be now?... Then the clergy and people would denounce the spiritual shackles and yoke and they would become more conscious and independent. They would not be ashamed of their Russian heritage, and would not depend on the kindness of the Irish biskup and the Spectator would not have had to complain that the priests are grabby and are uninformed. Instead - now there is a dominance of decay, division and disagreement!... And what has brought all this about? The naivete of the Uniate clergy, who imagined that Unia, in the eyes of the Catholic Church and its Pope, is a serious institution... Isn't that unfortunate? Isn't this unfortunate? Unia is the reason for all the disturbances and disorder! Isn't it the reason that there is no peace and order among Russians here? Thank the Lord! Even slowly we, the Orthodox people, are moving forward, even though there are great obstacles: the wickedness and the foolishness of some people!... One thing more - Spectator made a reference to Freeland... yes! The proverb "quis per quid peccatur, peridem etiam punitur"! was carried out on Rev. Fr. H. He was the first who submitted to the jurisdiction of a local biscup, he permitted his Russian church, built by the people, to be registered to the Roman-Catholic Irish biscup,- but then he was not careful and did not   pay his yearly quitrent cathedraticum   and the

Roman biscup used the reason that there was some disagreement among some of his parishioners and soon offered Fr. H. a blank resignation.

Concerning the property of the church, the Spectator said: "now all our church properties would
be composed into one good and strong organization" if, according to the words of Spectator,
the people and the priests would not only count their money. But what else should they have
counted, when there was nothing there? There was no newspaper and no school and nobody
knew the English language. Maybe Spectator thinks that during the ten years since the first
Uniate priest appeared here that two people could have taught all the people, who were for
centuries in spiritual darkness? Even the Spectator himself does not believe the contents of this
sentence. But let's assume, that some miracle happened, and everyone became Cicero or Kant
or Plato or someone similar: - even then Spectator by common sense should realize the nonsense of his words.

First: "we are not now subject to any authority, we ourselves have to make rules and that's
the end!" If the Spectator is a true son of the Uniate Church, then he should know that according to the Roman law, the people do not have any power or authority in the Church! Who is appointing and ordaining bishops for them? - The Pope! Ergo who will therefore, without
agreement of the Pope, obey Authorities elected by you? Even when Nicephor Chanath, under
the protection of the Papal delegate, was elected a Vicar, who accepted him as such?

Secondly, you do not want to be Orthodox and to submit to the jurisdiction of an Orthodox
bishop, - you also do not wish to acknowledge the Roman Catholic biskup, - and partially they you,
either... Therefore what kind of elected rule could there be? And of what faith would you then
be? Could it be that according to the American-Polish experience - you also would start "An Independent Holy Unia"? [108] Tertium non datur! - You do not find such assumptions idle talk? Do you
yourself seriously believe what you wrote? And to such rule you would have liked to register all
"church properties"? - or you would not? Then to whom? The property has to be registered to
someone, otherwise there can not be "one organization". To people? To church elders? It is
already partially registered now to them, but what purpose did it serve? What kind of church
properties are those, which have 10, 12 and even 25 thousand dollars of debt on them... Do
you think that if all these church properties were registered to the authority elected by you, that
then all these debts would be paid sooner? Who can guarantee, that this authority which has not
been approved by anyone, would not repeat the trick of A., and would not sell all deeds and
churches at an auction?

You do not like that the Orthodox and also the Catholic hierarchy demands that all properties be
registered to the Bishop? But according to my personal opinion, it is completely right: in the Orthodox Church the greatest ruling authority on earth is the - Bishop; - and in the Catholic - the
Pope. The biscup has only as much authority, e respectu jurisdictionis, as the Pope gives him.
In America the Council in Baltimore, according to the wish of the Pope, gave the right of oversee-
ing to the biskup.[109] If the Uniates are - true sons of the Pope, then they should register the Prop-

---

[108] *The Polish National Catholic Church of America was organized at Sranton, Pennsylvania, on
March 14, 1897, after long period of conflict between the Roman Catholic Bishops in America
and many Polish parishes. Poles, who had immigrated to the America around the turn of the
century objected that they had no bishops and only few priests who were Polish, that they
could not teach Polish in their parish schools and that according to the Council of Baltimore
in 1884 they had no right to establish Polish parishes of their own. Resentment smoldered
into open revolt against Irish bishops in America and resulted in the founding of an inde
pendent Polish Church in America. There were other national groups among Slovacs, Lithua-
nians, Carpatho-Russians and Hungarians that eventually have also broken away. Frank S.
Mead, Handbook of Denominations in the United States, Abingdon Press, Nashville, 1982,
pg. 203-204.

[109] "Americanism" - a crisis in American Catholic Church took its rise with Father Isaac Hecker
(1819-88), convert founder of the Paulists, who had forcibly maintained that American Catholics ought to develop their own techniques for convert making, with New World rather than
European environments in mind. By October, 1898, Pope Leo had personally intervened in
the dispute Leo XIII in his Testem Benevolentiae, January 22, 1899, made no doubt that
certain views, "called by some 'Americanism,'" deserved censure. The Pope asserted that "if
under the name of Americanism there should be designated the characteristic qualities which
reflected honor on the people of the United States, then there was no reason why these
should be questioned or discarded." Yet the Pope feared that there were "some among you

74

erties to the biskup, even more so since, the Uniate priests ask the Catholic biskup here for their jurisdiction. Upon meeting them the Uniate greet them with tambourines and trombones; they ask them to bless the cornerstones of their churches. The Orthodox people have to register the church properties to the Bishop also but they do it for other reasons. The Bishop in many places pays the salary of the clergy, supports the church, school, etc., etc., financially and therefore by law he must ask that! But here is the difference between them: the Orthodox people register the church properties to the Russian Orthodox Bishop, to their own Father's hands and it can never be lost. Even though some churches here in America might in the future for some reason cease to exist, the property would still remain in Orthodox Russian hands, and the Uniate property, registered to the biscup would remain with the Latin-Papists, who did nothing for the Uniates,- but even despised and persecuted them. Therefore, can't you tell that Unia is the main reason for the disturbances, disharmony and unhappiness?...

The biskup according to Catholic law and the wish of Pope, have authority over the Uniates, and they request only what they have a right to. Therefore why is it then that the majority of Uniate parishes does not want to acknowledge this; even though the Uniate priests pay their contributions to the biskup. It is also true that some of those Uniate parishes and priests at the same time tell, that they are under the authority of bishops in the Old Country. But can an educated priest seriously even think that? He knows himself and he teaches people, that the "Roman-Greek-Catholic faith" - is the same, he knows from the Papal bulls, teachings and decrees, that where there is no Greek-Uniate bishop, there the Uniates must be under the authority of a Catholic biscup. In America, Old Country bishops according to the spirit of the Papal Church, do not have jurisdiction, and consequently if anyone argues against this, then there are disturbances, disagreements and disorder. The Catholic biscup declares a Uniate priest who submits to an Old Country bishop as irregular, and even puts him under interdiction,- and if such a priest continues his activity, isn't it a tragedy? What is the reason for this?... Only Unia and always Unia!... There are also such Uniate priests here, who know that they can not be under the jurisdiction of the Old Country bishops, and do not acknowledge the local Catholic biskup - became "independent"... But can a priest be without a bishop, can he according to Church canons still function as a priest? Where does something like this happen? Only and exceptionally within Unia! The people, knowing that there no longer is a higher spiritual authority than the priest, started to introduce Presbyterian administration into their churches. Each one is a pope or bishop and gives orders to the priest, - is this situation normal? Is it demoralizing?

Then the Spectator says: "Orthodoxy does not differ in any way from Catholicism",- why? He gives us a wonderful explanation: "since one is absolutism and the other is also an absolutism!" Here is a method that can unite the churches. So many wise people were looking and breaking their heads! The contemporary infallible Vicar of Christ Leo XIII has devoted almost his entire life to this subject; he used all possible means, crafts, or according to the words of our dear organ, - made "promises". All this was done to unite the Ecumenical Church with his decaying, fallingapart Roman Church. And he did not succeed... And it is so easy and simple, that even Spectator overcame all the obstacles!... There is no difference between Papism and Orthodoxy - since "this is absolutism and that is also absolutism"! It is as clear as the egg of Columbus!... But, what form of administration would the Spectator like: constitutional, or republican, or anarchical? Or finally that, such as for example, the Uniate church has now in America? In otherwords, not to acknowl-

---

who conceive and desire a Church in America different from that which is in the rest of the world." The Pope pointed out that there is more authority and spiritual direction needed. Up until 1908 the American Catholic Church was under the missionary jurisdiction of the Congregation of Propaganda. There were up until then many conflicts with Rome to name some: - In 1846 the Council of Baltimore proclaimed the Immaculate Conception, 8 years before the dogma was proclaimed by Rome. Cardinal Gibbons was criticized for endorcing the Presidential Thanksgiving Day proclamation, the criticism for payment to the Holy See of 7 million dollars as compensation, for lands seized by the Aglipayans in the Philippine Islands etc. In 1884 the council in Baltimore prepared the Baltimore catechism which became a basic means of religious instruction in the U.S. In Rome there was criticism for ideological and nationalistic factions among the American Catholics, for Liberalism and participation in politics (Archbishop Ireland from Saint Paul, Minnesota as partisan at the Republican Party rallies). All these actions of American Catholic bishops do not show a very great dependence from the Pope but many disagreements with the Papal Church and Administration.

75

edge the Catholic biscup - and not to have one's own... that means not to have any authority! Everyone therefore has the right to participate in the Church and its administration; - the priest, according to Spectator, is a spiritual person, who has to "serve the liturgy", receive confessions and baptize. But from whom does the priest receive the authority to do that? From the authority above? - No, since that is "absolute authority", and Spectator doesn't wish such, he probably needs, if not republican, than constitutional authority for the parishioners. They will pay, accept or not the priest, and reader; they will support the church and church building, etc... Well! but who gives the priest the spiritual authority for religious services? A bishop? They do not have one, and it is not possible that they will have one, since he would have "absolute authority" from the Lord Christ Himself, who created His Church spilling His honest blood; the bishop was elected by the Holy Spirit... The Holy Spirit has no constitution, He does not ask the permission of parishioners when He selects a bishop for the administration of Christ's Church! Therefore, what will be the result? This is what!: the elders, the curators of the church, who are elected by all church members, will appoint an able person as president and then the president of the curators and the warden, himself in solidum with all curators will ordain the priest, and punctum! And that will be the "peoples'" constitutional, not appointed by "absolutism", priest! It will then be possible to talk with him wisely... it will be possible to remove him without difficulties at any time, whenever it would be wished... But it is strange in this case that the Spectator and these people from Galicia should permit the importing of people of "His Greatness'" status; since they were sent here by the absolute authority of the Cardinal-Metropolitan; who gave them also the authority for their clerical work here! Then why is it that Spectator et consortes do not ordain for themselves constitutional clerical authorities? "Sutome ultra crepidam!" Tailor - you have to stay with the thread! If someone knows as much about the Church administration, as does Spectator, then it would be better if he would keep quiet, and not exhibit himself to ridicule!

After all the remarks quoted above, Spectator said: "What hands pulled our people to Orthodoxy, what Grace awaits our people there?" - If he does not know the difference between Orthodoxy, Unia and Catholicism, then Orthodoxy will bring him as much Grace, as will Catholicism, and the main thing is that Orthodoxy "wishes the peoples' church properties" as much as does Catholicism.- Why does he then talk about the property, when he talks about about Unia as if it is some kind of a sect? If the property has such great significance in Spectator's opinion, then when did it happen that the Orthodox Church took the property away from the people? Then there would be the question, to whom should all these properties be registered to compose "one body" and besides, "that it would be well and strongly organized"? A body can be only where there is also a head... in the diocese the bishop is the head, - in the Ecumenical Church - Christ Himself, Who has promised to remain forever with His Church: He appoints the bishops through the Holy Spirit - and the Spectator wishes to have the people appoint the bishops to be constitutional administrators of the church properties and - "we will create for ourselves authority!" Is that not Presbyterian-Calvinist wisdom?... That's where Unia leads the Russian people, having such theologians, lawyers, leaders, and enlighteners as Spectator is! He admits also that Unia has only caused trouble for the Russian people, - but he is not ready to begin to use the only remedy - Orthodoxy! Is it better to form in America a Presbyterian-Uniate faith and church! But Spectator does not stop at this. Speaking about the Orthodox faith, he concludes that: to convince the Uniates, who are troubled Russian people wandering in the fog, that they should return to their great-grandfathers' only saving - the true - Church of Christ; - that is according to him only "our stereotype sentence repeated", since if "a search would be made among the great-grandfathers' faiths, we should all then return to paganism..." Here is where Spectator brought us with all his wisdom and made for himself an "unfading wreath" of glory"! It seems that Christianity and paganism is for him "wszystko jedno" (the same)! since paganism is older than Orthodoxy! That way for him any faith is good and leads to salvation, Christ and Jupiter, or Perun [110] - are all equal. Jupiter has then even superiority over Christ, since he was worshiped before! Millions have accepted him as god before the coming of God and Man!... Then all this "explanation" about administrations, churches, properties and other things, that Svoboda has presented to the Russian people in its "small topical satires" from the pen of Spectator becomes clear! It is very funny to read then also, that the Germans are mostly Protestants and

---

[110] *Perun was the chief god of the pagan Slavs in Eastern Europe; he was the god of thunder and the creator of fire.

do not plan to return to Catholicism. But why would they return? In what way is Roman-Catholicism better than Protestantism? Who was the reason for Protestantism? Was it not the Pope, who also started Unia? Having fallen away once from the true, Orthodox faith, and having separated himself from the Living Body of Christ, with his supporters, the Pope started a church that is not Christ's, but where he is venerated as the head; and naturally such a church should be separated and separated into smaller parts continuously, until it falls apart into atoms of godless, or indifferent people, for whom any faith would be fine and equal, that is according to Spectator, and according to the Pope - Spectator wish. You did not prove anything when you made a reference to the German-Protestants... I will show you also something: look at Protestant England, and at the Episcopalians in general, look what kind of desire they have to be closer to Orthodoxy, look at the German Old-Catholics, who made the first step toward the True Church of Christ.[111] Don't you know all that? But why would you have any reason to know it? For you the main concern is: to whom will the church properties be registered!... The rest - is fables. Naturally Spectator is right; if the American-Russian people will be offered several more of such "fly-traps" as this "small topical satire", and if they will believe them, then "certainly they will not run to Orthodoxy", but they will run to their destruction morally and spiritually! That's what you are teaching, - it is not enlightenment, - it is even worse than Unia. It is indifference, unbelief, and socialism, which was created in Galicia by Franko and the like, which was then imported by the Cardinal - patriots and by the propagation of Mount-Carmel's Svoboda. All this is the result of the decaying, pitiful condition of the unfortunate Unia!...

Concerning the condition of the American-Uniate church Spectator said: "there is now trouble, that is a fact. But where is there no trouble? Look around, Father Archpriest, for what has been happening for many years in San Francisco? Then look at Shepplon, Bridgeport, and maybe also at some of your other parishes. Only that at your places it happens quietly, by permission. But at our places it happens openly. When it boils - it has to boil over. The noise will go away; then the clear water will remain. These disturbances are not an "absolutely wonderful conclusion!" would say Spectator in the "Russian language". Mr. Orlov in "our dear organ" also acknowledges that there are problems and therefore, Spectator, we do not have to talk about that. But to refer to problems in other places and quasi by doing that to try to acquit the non-envious condition of Unia in America, and even more where it is, that is consolatio at lachrymas! And besides all this, there is a great difference between "problems"! Let's assume, that in some places, to which Spectator refers, there are or were problems and trouble, but the reason for them is not the system itself that is the matter, but it is the personalities! But in your troubles, Spectator, the entire essence of the matter is that Unia itself is the reason for problems. Where there is a bad foundation, there the building also continuously cracks and falls apart! Orthodoxy has as its foundation Christ-God Himself, it is based on the stone of faith, on the firm belief in the divinity of the Savior Jesus Christ! Therefore it will stay on earth until the end of time as the means of our salvation, and it will stay in spite of all persecutions, attacks, and tricks; Orthodoxy is not the cause of the problems, since Orthodoxy ex ipsa natura rei - has a good, - saving beginning. Can we say the same about Unia? Who can it name as its cornerstone? Sinful people, and traitors to Orthodoxy! And its main foundation is falsehood! It was invented not long ago, and it is supported by Jesuit-politic cunning. In places where these means lose their power, there Unia falls apart! Where else is Unia among the Russians? - In Austro-Hungary. What keeps it together? - Political considerations. If they end, then Unia will also be history. In America, politics does

---

[111] *For detailed information on the Anglican Church and Eastern Orthodox Church Union see the Annual Reports of the Union and the Russian-American Messenger 1903-1906. For the correspondence of the Orthodox Ecclesiastical Administration with the Old-Catholics see issues of the Russian American Messenger, 1903-1907.

A new ecumenical factor came into existence when the clergy of the Orthodox Church in America developed relations with Protestant and Catholic churches. Up until this time, Orthodoxy was not well understood in the West and was virtually unknown to Protestants. Anglicans, Old Catholics and other Church organizations made contacts with the Orthodox Church through the Orthodox Seminary in Minneapolis with Archbishop Tikhon and other Orthodox clergy in America. These contacts led to some cooperation and even plans for a united Christian Mission.

not need Unia, and it is dying, and it should die,- since the Russian people already "know how to think" - as Spectator said, and he said the truth. That is also the difference. You have mentioned San Francisco? What kind of a problem was there? Did Orthodoxy create the problem there?... No!... But-who? The nihilists and people, who live only to make life mean and unpleasant, who do not want to accept any authority, who like you wish to "make for themselves their own authority". And other malicious inventions are spread only by "Progress" - a newspaper printed by Jews - nihilists in New York. No one seriously considers the rumors spread by the newspaper except its accomplices - people from Russia and from Galicia. Was Orthodoxy hurt by their attacks? No; since their attacks, it began rapidly and victoriously to move across the mainland and it goes from the North to the East!... Shepplon?... A very funny matter? There one person suffers from human wickedness and he was removed because of that.[112] Was Orthodoxy hurt because of that? - No! not even one person was lost, despite all the Jesuit-Uniate tricks that were used, the purchase of the "deed" for the church property and all possible and impossible various Uniate tricks, that the Uniates wanted to use; making certain references to the not praise worthy weakness of a person, the pastor of that church. In the end, the person who caused all the harm, returned to Unia?... Bridgeport? But what special happened there? The centuries-old hostility between Slovaks and Hungarians, even though they were of the same faith, children of the same church, began among them and and the result was that today there are in Bridgeport not one, but two Orthodox churches, Slavic and Hungarian. Was Orthodoxy because of that hurt? No!... But, if some troubles are ignited - which happens very seldom, they can be explained by two reasons:-

1) People in America who reunited, - naturally a smaller group - were already used to the Uniate-constitutional form of parish administration; that is they wished to give orders as before, to support the Uniate lawlessness. This is their "potestas a se et in se" , about which Spectator dreams, and this condition can not be permitted,- we have a bishop, that means that one, whom the Uniates do not have,- and since we have one, we have to obey him. We can not say "we will chase the priest out", or "we will close the church to him". The Orthodox clergy in America exists for the people, but they are servants of the Church. They are not slaves who are subordinated to the people,- therefore, they have to report not to the people, but to God and the bishop. How important is the bishop for the Church? I will not even speak about that subject which has been discussed very much already by "Svoboda" and "our dear organ" together with "our dear Union". "Our dear Union" is completely convinced, that if the Uniates would receive a bishop, then all disagreements would stop among them... I do not negate this idea in principio, but will repeal, that all disturbances among the Uniates will stop no sooner than when they will stop being Uniates, and will subordinate themselves to the authority of an Orthodox bishop.- A Uniate bishop in America is a "nonsense"! He would be here, if he would come, without any authority and power! The Roman Catholic Irish hierarchy would treat him in the same way as they treat the Uniate clergy, consequently his own flock would not respect him as he should be respected. This poor man, would on his forehead carry an insignia of blame!

2) If in an Orthodox parish disturbances begin, a Uniate ksendz could be found somewhere around: probably he went around there with Papal teaching and water from Lourdes and other nonsense!

As it is, Mr. Spectator could show three places where, according to him, there were disturbances in Orthodox parishes. But if we look for support in statistics, then our illustration will be more expressive. Let's begin: a) Brooklyn, b) Passaic, c) Yonkers, d) Jersey-City, e) Hazleton, f) Mac Adoo, g) Freeland, h) Scranton, i) Olyphant, j)Shenandoah, k) Philadelphia, L) Cleveland, m) Trenton, n) Streator, o) New York, p) Kingston, r) Duquesne. And what kind of matters happened there and are still going on? I suppose Spectator doesn't want them listed; otherwise it would be necessary to write whole books about them, and there would be facts that would be supported by witnesses,- not by rumors as were in "Progress", in "Svoboda" and in "Our dear Organ". "That person" is very interested in all glorious and not so glorious deeds of the American Rus' especially by the leaders. Therefore:

3) Quid hoc at tantam sitim! I suggest to Spectator not to get involved with statistics, because I can convince him that he, not I will lose.

---

[112] * The priest there had a drinking problem and was replaced

The conclusion that follows from all this is: if the American-Russian people wish happiness for themselves, to better their contemporary fate,- they have first of all - to leave the cause of all their troubles - Unia - and to return to the only Saving Faith and to the Church of Christ, the Orthodox, since it is the only True One and it is their Church. It supports them, gives power, teaches and loves its nationality. In the past centuries it made them strong, mighty and glorious, and when they left it, they became weak-willed slaves! God has left them, giving them over to their enemies!... They must against the suggestions of Spectator return to their Mother - The Holy Orthodox Church, otherwise they will be lost forever, especially if they will be instructed in radicalism and socialism by "Svoboda" and Spectators", and "our dear organ" who all systematically lead them to foolishness and darkness!...

I have finished, and I want only to add: Yes! "This person" is very interested in matters of the American Church and people, and without exaggeration, without boasting, with a clear conscience he can tell, that he knows better than anyone the situation of the American-Russian people. With surprise he looks at those who could lead the people to the easier road of salvation, who purposely close that road to them, who create clouds in front of them, and prevent the people in their good intentions.

The Greek-Catholic Union

On the 29th of October, 1890, in Wilkes-Barre, Pensylvania the Greek-Catholic priests who have been in the United States met and among everything else they have been there consulting, what would be the best way to start the fraternities, and to unite all of them into one;- the meeting delegated Father Alexis Toth who was the president of the meeting, at that time the spiritual father in Minneapolis, that for the goal of unity of the Greek-Catholic fraternities he would send a circular appeal to all existing fraternities, which he also did, by 6-18 December, 1890, he sent the appeal, in Slovak language, since there was not a Russian printshop.[113] The goal of uniting all the fraternities has been:

1) to preserve the interests of the Eastern-Russian Church, its rites since the Catholic biskups did not want to accept the Greek-Catholic priests.[114] And they have been so hostile to them, have been even excommunicating them, and have been making personal statements against them,- and mainly it was done because, the Greek-Catholic priests a) have been performing the sacrament of the anointing, b) they gave communion to their faithful in both forms[115] c) they are - married,- and according to Catholic opinion that was horror - and a "scandal"!

2) to preserve the Russian nationality, since many fraternities were joining alien organizations, or Russians were joining alien fraternities, and also foreign to Russian people - unions, and finally

3) to give aid to the sick and widows, and also to orphans; in other words, the insurance of the members in case of death. The goals as it is seen, were very nice and praiseworthy.- "The Union" of Russian-Greek-Catholic fraternities was formed in the same Wilkes-Barre by the second appeal of Father Theofan Obushkievich in 1891,- and as its president was elected Ivan A. Zhinchak-Smith a salesman from Mahanoy-city Pennsylvania.- But at the forming of the "Union" there was made a mistake which in no way was wished to be made by the priests of the first meeting in Wilkes-Barre,- at the formation of the Union it was expressed, that in the "Union" could be accepted also - Roman Catholics! And in that way the former goals of the "Union" were contradicting - since the consulting priests in Wilkes-Barre on the 29 th of October were wishing and planning to

---

[113] There was a printshop in Shenandoah of the "Russkoe Slovo", but its owner Andruk hovich' was an enemy of all good deeds.

[114] De Propagande Fide appeared to agree to send the Uniate priests to America but has been sending secret instructions to the local biskups,- especially Cardinal Simeoni,- that the local biskups would in any way hinder the activity of the Uniate priests.

[115] However Roman Catholic Church laymen received communion only under one species; that of bread, and only ordained priests take it under both species.

form a strictly Russian organization; - and through that later it came so out, that the "Union", from the moment of its formation has had to struggle against "Katolic Jednota"! since many Greek-Catholic fraternities joined that "Roman-Catholic" organization.- And it has to be acknowledged that the "Union" in their organ "Amerikanskii-Russkii Viestnik" - in that case very justfully-called on those Russian fraternities, that they would join their own, and not an alien organization, and because of that, "Jednota" began to attack angrily, and sharply, and even badly the "Union"; - and in that it was also getting aid from the Ukrainophils' "Russkoe Slovo" printed in Shenandoah whose editor was the notorious and vindictive exksendz Andrukhovych', who because of his private hate and his spiritual lowness to his own co-brothers, was ready not only to harm everything, which they wanted to do beneficial, but even - to destroy everything!- "the Union" as it could - but quietly was defending itself in its organ "Viestnik", however forgetting, that it suffers the same fault as "Jednota" that is,- that they were accepting in their membership Roman Catholics.[116] The other and even greater guilt of the Union was, that the "Union" namely was formed for working people, and the prime place there had to be taken by the people,- but what happened? Greek Catholic (Uniate) clergy,- for what reason? and on what grounds?- took the business matters of the Union, for example at the main convention all priests who were there had all right to speak, if they were delegates or not? And out of that followed, that the priests made of the Union some kind of a supreme church spiritual authority, and at conventions, at so called "officer meetings" there was talked more about the faith, about the parishes, about personal and private interests, than about the matters of the "Union" and about- people! The "Union" started to form such church spiritual authority and tribunal especially from the time, when the Greek Catholic clergy after several different (multiple) and (in vain) requests - first to "old country bishops",- then to Rome, then to the Papal delegate Satolli, and they could not, and they can't get a biskup for America, or at least even an "apostolic vickery";[117] And it could have happened only in that way that, at the first "supreme convention" held in Scranton in 1893 on the 30th of May on the demand of the priests the convention with however insignificant a majority of votes, excluded - crossed out the fraternity of Wilkes-Barre from the "Union", because it united with their grandparental faith and the Orthodox Church, or according to the Uniate dictionary as it was said, that the members of the fraternity became "schismatic", accepting "Muscovite(!?) faith!" In vain they were reminded by one priest, who recently came from Europe, that they would not do such foolishness, because this is not the business of the "Union" but nothing could have been done against foolishness and fanaticism!... The priests achieved what they wanted!...

The third and even greater fault of the "Union" was that, the same priests who took in their hands the control of the "Union" instead that they would as it was planned as the main goals of the "Union", preserve the Eastern rite, and Russian nationality, have been looking that they would achieve the "kindness and favor" of the local Catholic biskups - and they were calling on Catholic biskups and have been meeting them with drums and music, have been bowing to them, let them register the churches in their name, have been calling them for the blessing of the cornerstones of the churches, the bells, the iconostasis... in other words their motto has been "to vsicko jedno" [118] - now how can any right thinking person; how can any right thinking person; how can the people join their own, or how he would love his own, support his own, if he sees, that his - Eastern, Russian rite church, his iconostasis a biskup is blessing in Latin, in infula!... In this way the spiritual fathers every time have been showing their people and show now the superiority of the Roman Latin church,- and even more: Cornelius Laurisin has clearly said it in "Svoboda".-[119] Because of that it is not surprising to anyone, why not only in Europe, but even here are many ashamed of their Russian nationality, of their Eastern rite!... And what is even more confusing the

---

[116] The editor of "Jednota", even though he was from Hungary, in Hungarian Russian Uniate priests saw "muscovites" and "schismatics".

[117] It is a funny matter! If Roman Catholics only have 20-40 parishes, they immediately hope that the Pope would appoint for them a biskup or an "apostolicus vicarius"... but the Uniates, those dear children of his could hardly get a biskup in Europe when they had 200-300 parishes... and here in America he doesn't even want to hear about it.

[118] to vsicko jedno - Polish - it's the same.

[119] However this was what he has been studying "the theology" for...? The poor fellow is convinced that he is existing only ex favente gratia of the Pope!...

minds is the circumstance, that many priests are clearly or secretly aspiring to be - biskups, and hold themselves only as earned candidates to the biskupric, and they have their own friends, who at the cost of others, also candidates are secretly intriguing, and who form "groups", and among themselves they are conducting a secret fight; and to that it is necessary also to know; that there are priests from 3 dioceses: from Lvov, from Priashev and from Mukachevo;- for those who are from Lvov (Galicians) the people from Priashev and Mukachevo are "Hungarians",- to the people from Priashev and Mukachevo - the Galicians are "Polacks"! And among the people from Priashev and Mukachevo there is also hostility and disagreement; [120] now, how there could be even expected, and even could be thought about honorable cooperation for those church and national goals, which were taken to the program of the "Union"? It is even laughable to hear how many times have these spiritual fathers met with the goal of "interests of the common good" (this is their beloved sentence). How can they make among themselves peace, agreement, brotherly love,- when even "the sacred Spolok under the protection of the holy Apostle Andrei the First Called" which was formed last year in Hazleton and this year in Olyphant, as soon as they formed it began there hostility, intrigue, disagreements, suspicions even more among them!... first secretly, then clearly - even in the newspapers!... and these people want to create happiness and to lead the "American Rus"!...

But the worst service was made to the "Union" by those, what mostly hurt and is hurting the "Union" - by those, who founded the "Union", decided to publish an organ (newspaper) for the American Russians!... at the cost of the Union! Certainly such an organization as the "Union" could not and cannot be without an organ (newspaper), especially here in America, and it is not here a mistake,- but first they decided to print it at the cost of the "Union", which did not have yet any funds for the printing house and to do so the funds have had to be either borrowed, or the money which was given to the "Union" for other purposes, be used for the printing house;- then, instead, that one of the priests would become editor of the organ (newspaper) since the organ "Amerikanskii Russkii Viestnik" since it is the organ not only of the "Union", but also it is the official Organ of the Greek Catholic Clergy of the U.S.A. as it calls itself,- but no they gave the editorship to the ex-notorious who didn't have any knowledge about the editing of a newspaper and who just came from Europe, and who did not know Russian and English languages and even until today does not know, and who immediately started to write in some kind of a funny- Ethiopian African language [121] long articles, that neither he, nor the subscribers could understand,- who started to praise his own personality, to clear it and to wash it in the organ; cursing, starting unreasonable polemics, who reported and is reporting attacks,- and who wrote about "our dear Union" such glorious news glorifying it that the person who didn't understand the internal glorifying it that the person who didn't understand the internal matters, thought that the "Union" swims in oil and in honey,- about "our lawful spiritual father" has been reporting such "glorifications" that it could be thought, that among "our lawful spiritual fathers" there are St. John Chrysostom, St. Gregory, St. Basil, St. Afonasy, in other words, according to the "articles" and "correspondence", there is Paradise in the Union and "the Union" is in the center of Paradise!... It is true that immediately after the first "main convention" there started to spread some kind of unpleasant news about the "Union",- but the sponsors of the "Union" however put the fire out, [122] but they didn't put it out for long because in a little while in Shamokin, Pennsylvania there was founded "Russkii Narodnyi Soyuz", whose goal has been to unite the Russians by nationality, not depending on their faith,- and it was said very well, and possibly "Soyuz" would even blossom today if it would not be from the beginning secretly, and then obviously as it's said express its "Russianity", by making plans here in America "to create a little Ukraine" and the organ of the "Soyuz"- "Svoboda" started to talk about "Czar glorifying", about "Muscovite hirelings" about "disunited Russian people" and in such way as to disunite here the Russian people!... But in vain! The Pigulacks, Stolskis, Dragomanovs, Vachnianins, Barvinskis - will not find in America fools and Frankos even less,- the Galicians and Hungarian Russian people who came here, know that they are Russian, and

---

[120] The fish starts to smell from the head. The diocese of Mukachevo has always been like a "patron" of the Priashev diocese.

[121] Ethiopian African - i.e. a funny, unintelligible language.

[122] The first attack against the Union came from Bridgeport, Connecticut.

that the Great Russian people - are their own brothers! They do not want to know anything about the "Ukraine" and about "Ukrainophils"!...

As soon as "Soyuz" started its activity, the organ of "our dear Union", "that is Viestnik", smelled also over there "schism"! And there started polemics, arguments, between the 2 organs and they were great. It has to be known, that the editor of the "Viestnik" has a wonderful fantasy that can be in the best way called a "horse fantasy" [123] who started to make impossible lies, twisting, who stirred people up and cursing! Naturally "Svoboda" used the same "decency" against "Viestnik"! and this "activity" should have been for the use of the - "American Rus'"!... and even that "Viestnik", as it has been said about, "our dear Union" wrote the best about it and its glorifying did not have any result, in "our dear Union" something has been rotting and from here came some kind of unpleasant smell!... And that has been smelled and felt also by the organ of the Union's "Viestnik" and because of that it started to look for reasons for that rotting condition! It exerted, strained its "horse fantasy" and some how from "Above" it received "inspiration" and it declared to the entire world, that there is no other reason for the rotting than "schism" and "itinerant disciples"!... And there appeared a "circular letter" with a funny contents! It was fabricated by the wisdom of the editor of "Viestnik", approved by the authority of our "lawful priest", and signed by Ivan R. Smith and in such a way it appeared to the world! What kind of endless stupidity, contradiction, inconsequential, twisting of historical facts there has been invented, it was all put down on paper and published in the "circular letter" there is only one funny thing in that circular letter story and it is even not understandable why the president of "our dear Union" Mr. Smith gave his name to it? Why those who did "praise" or not, who wrote the circular letter?... After the circular letter there came a whole "golden horde" of confusing most wise articles in "Viestnik" against the "schism" and against the "itinerant disciples", who however existed in the empty head of the editor even until today, these articles have been differing from the circular letter in that their stupidity has been greater - there has been cursing, and absence of "elementary decency" and "with such articles" "our dear Union" with the help of "our organ Viestnik" has been teaching and enlightening - the American Rus'!... Unwillingly every normally thinking person has to ask what for and why the organ of "our dear Union" has been occupied not with the matters of "the Union", why it attacked and cursed others,- why it did not teach the Russian people about their glorious past, about the glorious and clear days of the Russian nation, why he didn't write for the Russian people about its unhappiness, about its suffering, about its patience? If "our dear Union" wished and wanted to teach and to enlighten the American Russian people,- then to do that it cannot find a more suitable time and place - as now here in the free America! Then why the American Russian people have to be fooled, blackened, disunited with such stupid fables as "schism"- "itinerant disciples" etcetera, etcetera? Now everyone knows about it, so that nobody would ask about internal matters of "our Union", how "our dear Union" is managing, going, and that since in "our dear Union" the matters are not going well, something has been rotting there... the people have been told, that the only reason for it is "schism" and "itinerant disciples"!...

But the matters could not be hidden and made secret; especially it could not be hidden that, the organ of "our dear Union", "Viestnik" costs very much, and because of it in 1894 a committee elected by the "Union" has had to announce, that the organ - "Viestnik" - cannot be printed at the cost of the "Union",- because it will eat up all the money of the Union,- and it will not bring any usefulness to the "Union" itself and then it was decided, to give over the organ to the editor that he would not only edit but also print the organ, and for that he will be paid by the Union $50 monthly! And the expenses for the printing the editor would pay himself!... It has to be told also, that the organ "Viestnik" that began to enlighten the American Rus' from Mahanoy-city with its "light of wisdom" after the first convention has been transferred to Scranton and then even more it didn't appear in Scranton too long and "the clear sunshine" and "the shimmering light" - and "base", "spiritual head" of the American Rus', moved there where has been "the temporary manager" of the American Greek Catholic Church for the present, past, and future time, he, the long time candidate for the biskupric, the almighty pan!... [124]

---

[123] • "horse fantasy" - In Russian, this means that the person has a very strong imagination.

[124] • Father Alexis refers to Nicephor Chanath.

At the conventions

The past month of May, especially the last two weeks of May, was the time of all kinds of conventions,- namely; "Amerikansko-Slovensky Narodny Spolok" held its 4 th convention in Wilkes-Barre; "Zivena" the female fraternity of Slavic women held its 2 nd convention also in Wilkes-Barre;- the "Russian Orthodox Catholic Mutual Aid Society" held its 2nd convention in Allegheny city, Pa.; the "GREEK-Catholic Fraternity Union"- held its 4 th convention in Braddock, Pa., the "Evangelsca Luteranska Jednota" held its 2 nd convention in Bridgeport, Conn., and in the month of June the "Pennsylvanska Rimo i GRECO-Katolicha Jednota" held its 4 th convention in Wilkes-Barre, Pa.

All those - are Slavic and Russian fraternities and brotherhoods... And it is very comforting to read about them that they are all active and useful to the Slavic people,- the thought is also comforting, that the Slavic nations here in the land of freedom have come to an awareness of the need of national and church unity and they have worked in that direction!...

Of those organizations: 1) "Amerikansko-Slovensky Narodny Spolok", 2) Zivena and 3) Russkii Narodnyi Soyuz are "nationalistic" organizations,- who accept members of differing faiths,- 4) the Russian Orthodox Catholic Mutual Aid Society, 5) the Evangelsca Luteranska "Jednota", 6) Pennsylvanska Rimo i GRECO-Katolicha Jednota and 7) GREEK-Catholic Fraternity Union,- besides nationality take into consideration also faith and are religious organizations.- Concerning membership the matter stands like this:

1) Amerikansko-Slovensky Narodny Spolok has around 9000 members
2) Zivena   2000
3) Russkii Narodnyi Soyuz   1100
4) Russian Orthodox Catholic Mutual Aid Society   750
5) Katholicka Slovenska Jednota   1000
6) Pennsylvanska Rimo i GRECO-Katolicha   1800
7) GREEK-Catholic Fraternity Union   5200

All together about 20,000 people of Slavic-Russian nationality are united here in America!

The convention of Amerikansko-Slovensky Narodny Spolok", was really wonderful especially the parade through the city of Wilkes-Barre, in which also "Zivena" took part,- the parade stretched for more than a mile and more than 2000 members took part; the streets along which the marchers passed, were decorated with American and Slavic - including Russian, - flags; the local English newspapers reported very positively about our Slavic brothers. In this much credit deserves the founder of this Spolok Mr. Piotr V. Rovnianek due to the fact of his indefatigable work in America not only among Slovaks, but also other Slavs. "Amerikansko-Slovensky Narodny Spolok" keeps in front of the eyes the All-Slavic unity, this was proved during the convention; many members and delegates even though by faith non-Orthodox, appeared in large numbers for Devine services in the local Orthodox church and even elected as an honorary member the pastor of the Wilkes-Barre Orthodox church Archpriest A.G. Toth.

The awareness of the unity of the Slavs was shown also by the delegates of the Russian Orthodox Catholic Mutual Aid Society, who by the way personally visited the glorious champion of the Slovak Mr. Rovnianek in Pittsburgh, but the Evangelsca Luteranska "Jednota" did not lag behind, showing their friendly relations with the pastor of the Russian Orthodox Church in Bridgeport, Father M. Bologh. Herewith "A.S. N. Spolok", "Zivena", the Russian Orthodox Catholic Mutual Aid Society and the Evangelsca Luteranska "Jednota" indeed showed, that their members are the children of one Slavic family and their relations were and are everywhere friendly and brotherly!.. But what can we say about the others?.. It is sad even to think, not only to speak!..

As is seen from the name: Pennsylvanska Rimo i GRECO-Katolicha Jednota - also has a membership of Russian nationality,- by faith Uniate! Those poor people are so demoralized, that they are ashamed of the Russian name and to the question: what nationality are you, persistently would repeat, that they are "Greek-Catholics" they would not admit their Russian nationality for anything! They have received an order (it is even hard to believe), that God protects them during the convention to go to the Orthodox church (according to the Catholic-Uniate terminology "schismatic or Muscovite"), otherwise they would be fined or thrown out of the Jednota!.. so what can be done? The obedient "Greek-Catholic" Uniate obeys his pan!

In "Soyuz" according to the Ukrainophils' newspaper "Svoboda", business proceeded quite objectively, nevertheless above everything else there was "Russianity" dominating, quite socialistic and radical ad normam "leaders of the Russian nation" of the type of Franko, [125] and other luminaries of the radical-Socialist Party, that today little by little begins to spread in Galicia. It is funny only that, the Uniate ksendzes are flirting with those ideas here also, forgetting that, for Franko's ideas they may pay bitterly not only in Galicia, but also mainly here in America! We cannot think about the "enlightenment" - without a religious base,- and most important it cannot even be thought, that Franko et tutti quanti with their alleged "enlightenment" would ever give to the Russian people, whose faith and nationality are so strongly tied together and the soul with the body, that, which they are taking away from them by pushing them from the faith and the church!.. The Russian person without faith, and most important without the Orthodox faith, is a - dead corpse, a soulless body: it was quite proved by the history of the Russian nation.

The Russian Orthodox Catholic Mutual Aid Society without noise and without demonstration conducted quietly their convention but with the consciousness and comfort, that this organization is among all Slavic-Russian organizations the youngest one,- only just 2 years old,- doesn't have any difficulties, has paid considerably and fully the posthumous benefits,- and besides this has a $ 2,000 reserve fund!

The "GREEK-Catholic Fraternity Union" among all the named organizations had the most turbulent convention. To understand the reason for this, it is necessary to know the past events in that organization. This can be learned in the best way from the pamphlet "What Is Happening in the Neighbor's Hut"! [126]

As soon as the delegates of the convention came together the motto was already announced - "Away with the Priests", it was the Uniate clergy, who occupied the Union, who became dominant there, not for the profit of the people, but for their own profit! Because of that, it happened at the convention that not even one of them was elected as an officer, with the exception of the inspector of the "organ" the newspaper "Am. R. Viestnik", and also after the elections; a pure-blooded Hungarian, was elected as a secretary, one who had become during 4-5 months a Uniate from a Calvinist, by first of all marrying the daughter of the editor of the Uniate "Viestnik", and secondly, to be able to be elected as the secretary! Horrible scenes happened during the meeting; one of them almost didn't end with that, the notorious "speaker" and ksendz had wanted to arrest a delegate by "warrant" who said to him among other things, that he as a Russian priest cannot even read nor write in Russian! The importance of the matter and the "comicum" is that, this was said by the Calvinist- who had been metamorphosed into a Uniate!

It would be a blank survey of the events of the convention, if it would be silent about, the inaugurated doctor from Cleveland S. Sabov who held or according to the words of "Viestnik"- "proclaimed" a sermon in the church: with an unusual that is with a "doctoral" wisdom thundering against the "schismatics", so that even the walls were cracking and the river Monongahela "turned back": the delegates have been very satisfied with a sermon that had not head nor tail, even that they did not understand it fully, and the luminary doctor was also very satisfied with his oratorical success!

Among the decisions of the convention can be found also, that several members as a deputation will go to Washington, to the Papal delegate, and if they will not be successful in reaching their goal, than they will swim to Rome, to Priashev, to Uzhorod,- maybe also to Peking, to Kozurkov and so on but they have to bring a biskup- that is the goal! - alive or half-dead, but

[125] *Franko, Ivan Iakovlevich, (1856-1916). A Western Ukrainian writer, poet, critic and activist. He was born in a farm family, studied in the Universities of Lvov and Vienna and propagandized the ideas of Russian-Revolutionary Democracy and then Marxism. He spoke for the unity of Ukrainians paying for this with three jail sentences and with persecutions. He translated works of Marx and Engels publicizing their ideas among workers. He also edited magazines.

[126] *A pamphlet published by Father Alexis in 1896 containing four articles: "The Greek Catholic Union"; "The Church Lawsuit in Wilkes-Barre"; "Episodes From The Trial" and "The War of the Frogs (Toads) Against the Mice".

he must be there.. Naturally the commission or committee will make this excursion at the expense of the members of the Union. The Grand Pan will again compose a Memorandum,- it seems that it is already the 8th Memorandum, which will probably go there for its eternal peace where its predecessors went to the Vatican there where the "Infallible Vicar" goes on fool! [127]

Among all the organizations the "Union" is paying the most liberally to their officers: the editor receives in a year $1200, the secretary $ 600, the Inspector of the "organ" $ 300, the treasurer $ 250,- this means that just the eadership of the Union needs altogether $ 2325! Besides this the secretary and the inspector, if they travel for the business of the Union, then they receive $ 4 a day for expenses! The property of the Union, including the printing house, including the editor, the furniture, the shelves, the unsold calendars, etc., is about $ 4000!! The debts are over $ 4000,- and the invention of the editor of "Viestnik" and the "Emergency Iron Fund" has about $ 600,- now let everyone himself calculate, how much property the Union has after 5 years!

Comparing the "Russian Orthodox Catholic Mutual Aid Society" with the Union we will also learn that in the Society the members of the convention have elected priests as even the president, as a secretary and as editor! and in the Union the spiritual fathers received a - laufpass! [128]

In the "Union" a new officer position has been created, that of a confessor for the "Union", for this important position was elected the luminary "doctor" from Cleveland: he now breaks his head about the matter, what kind of obligations he has in conjunction with this position, since every fraternity of the Union has its own confessor! Oh, it doesn't matter! Mundus titilis titulaturi! Our doctor can help the others "mit Rat und That" [129] so he can help himself also.

Finally it is said also that the Uniate spiritual fathers have mercifully decided to stay in the Union for a year or even for 2 for a "test", and if the consequences will show, that the "chlops" [130] will not be able to run the "Union" then they will be ready again to "sacrifice" themselves for that matter, and if the "chlops" can do without them, then the "confessors", will join en masse the Catholic "Jednota"... What is truthful in this matter is not known, but as a matter of fact, one of the "original" activists of the Union the ksendz Cornelius Laurisin already left the Union! And the other fact is that, Ivan Andreevich Zhinchak-Smith, whom the ksendzes had intended to throw out of office, pushed them himself from the Union in a "peasant way", and the third fact is that the president of the Union is swat [131] of the editor and the editor is again test' [132] of the secretary, and the secretary, finally, is ziat' [133] of the editor, and so the business of the Union is patriarchal-nepotistical and so the matter of the Union will go in a patriarchal-nepotistical way... Lieb Vaterland mag'st ruhig sein! [134] Oh, God give it for many and good years!..

---

[127] "A Russian saying meaning even the Pope who is usually carried everywhere walks to the bathroom.

[128] laufpass - German - discharge papers.

[129] mit Rat und That - German - to help with suggestions and deeds. (In word and deed)

[130] chlops - Polish and Ukrainian - meaning peasants.

[131] swat - Russian - father of the son-in-law or of the daughter-in-law.

[132] test' - Russian - father-in-law.

[133] ziat' - Russian - son-in-law or brother-in-law.

[134] Lieb Vaterland... - German - Dear Fatherland you can be reassured.

www.ingramcontent.com/pod-product-compliance
Lightning Source LLC
Chambersburg PA
CBHW021418090426
42742CB00009B/1179